Out of Africa II

Authors Notes

When deciding to do this series, I didn't want to just design ordinary coloring books like so many others out there do, I wanted mine to be different. I wanted mine to be educational, and to cover all ages from children to adults. My goal is to teach people about some of the different animals you can find within the country of South Africa, and that is just for starters. After this coloring book is released, I will be venturing into other countries as well, including here in the United States, where I live. That is the first country now on my list. In creating these coloring books, I wanted to raise awareness of the plight of some of the endangered animals that need help, and maybe even instill a curiosity in some way that will make you want to learn more about the animals that you are coloring. Only when we care about the animals, will we try to help the animals. And for some that are on the endangered species list...the help can't come soon enough.

All illustrations and depictions of the animals within this coloring book are the sole possession of the author. No part of this book may be reproduced, stored in a retrieval system, or transmitted by any means without the expressed written permission of the author. The author of this coloring book is not a professional artist, nor does she claim to be. With that being said, all the drawings contained within the pages of this book were entirely hand~drawn by the author, and no computerized images or graphics were used to produce them.

Cover Design By: BJ LaPier

Out of Africa II

The "Out of Africa II" educational coloring book is dedicated to all those who work and devote their lives to protecting Animals all over the world. Poaching and big game trophy hunting are just two of the dangers facing animals everywhere throughout the world. In Africa, humans are directly causing the possible extinction of entire species. There may come a day when seeing these majestic animals in the wild will no longer exist. The only place to see them will be in zoos, picture books, museums or in the various wildlife documentaries on TV. We need to do what we can to preserve what we have now, we need to take care of the animals that are left in the wild, and stop taking away the habitat that they need to live and thrive in. No animal should ever be killed just for its mount, horns, ivory or fur. It is just wrong.

A big Thank You also goes out to the whole staff of Wild Earth, the presenters, the camera men and the people who are behind the scenes, past, present and future. Without them, this educational African themed coloring book, and any future African Themed educational coloring books that may be produced, would not have been possible. A special Thank You goes out to Mr. Graham Wallington and his wife, Emily. Without this couple, Wild Earth would not exist. Wild Earth was their brain~child, and now thousands of people around the entire world can tune in and enjoy seeing and experiencing what a real~live African Safari would be like. Twice daily, a live interactive safari takes place via the web. Professional Guides escort you out into the African bush to show you animals of all kinds, both big and small. Djuma Research Center, in the Kruger National Park, is home base for Wild Earth. Over the past two years though, Wild Earth has been expanding to cover other areas in Africa as well. Currently they are broadcasting from not only Djuma, but from the Kalahari, Kenya and elsewhere. The link below will help you find these live interactive safaris' if you would like to tune in and watch, I know you won't be sorry!

To watch the live, interactive Wild Earth safaris, please to their youtube channel at:

https://www.youtube.com/channel/UCV6HJBZD_hZcIX9JVJ3dCXQ

BLEED SHEET

CAREFULLY CUT THIS SHEET OUT AND PLACE IT BETWEEN YOUR PAGES AS YOU COLOR. THIS WILL HELP TO ENSURE THAT THE COLORS OF THE PREVIOUSLY COLORED SHEETS WILL NOT RUB OFF ONTO THE BACKSIDE OF WHAT YOU ARE CURRENTLY WORKING ON.

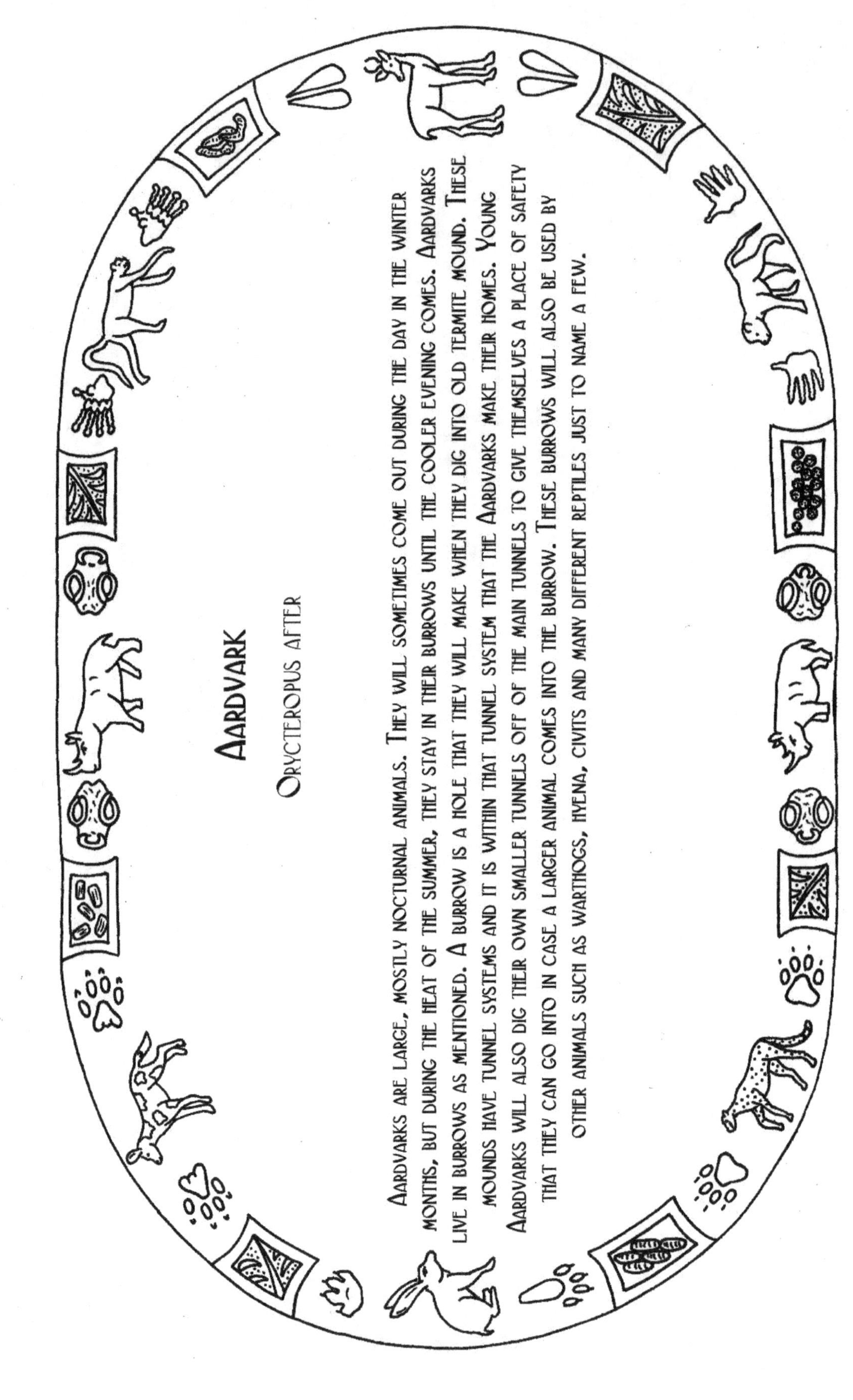

Aardvark

Orycteropus After

Aardvarks are large, mostly nocturnal animals. They will sometimes come out during the day in the winter months, but during the heat of the summer, they stay in their burrows until the cooler evening comes. Aardvarks live in burrows as mentioned. A burrow is a hole that they will make when they dig into old termite mound. These mounds have tunnel systems and it is within that tunnel system that the Aardvarks make their homes. Young Aardvarks will also dig their own smaller tunnels off of the main tunnels to give themselves a place of safety that they can go into in case a larger animal comes into the burrow. These burrows will also be used by other animals such as warthogs, hyena, civits and many different reptiles just to name a few.

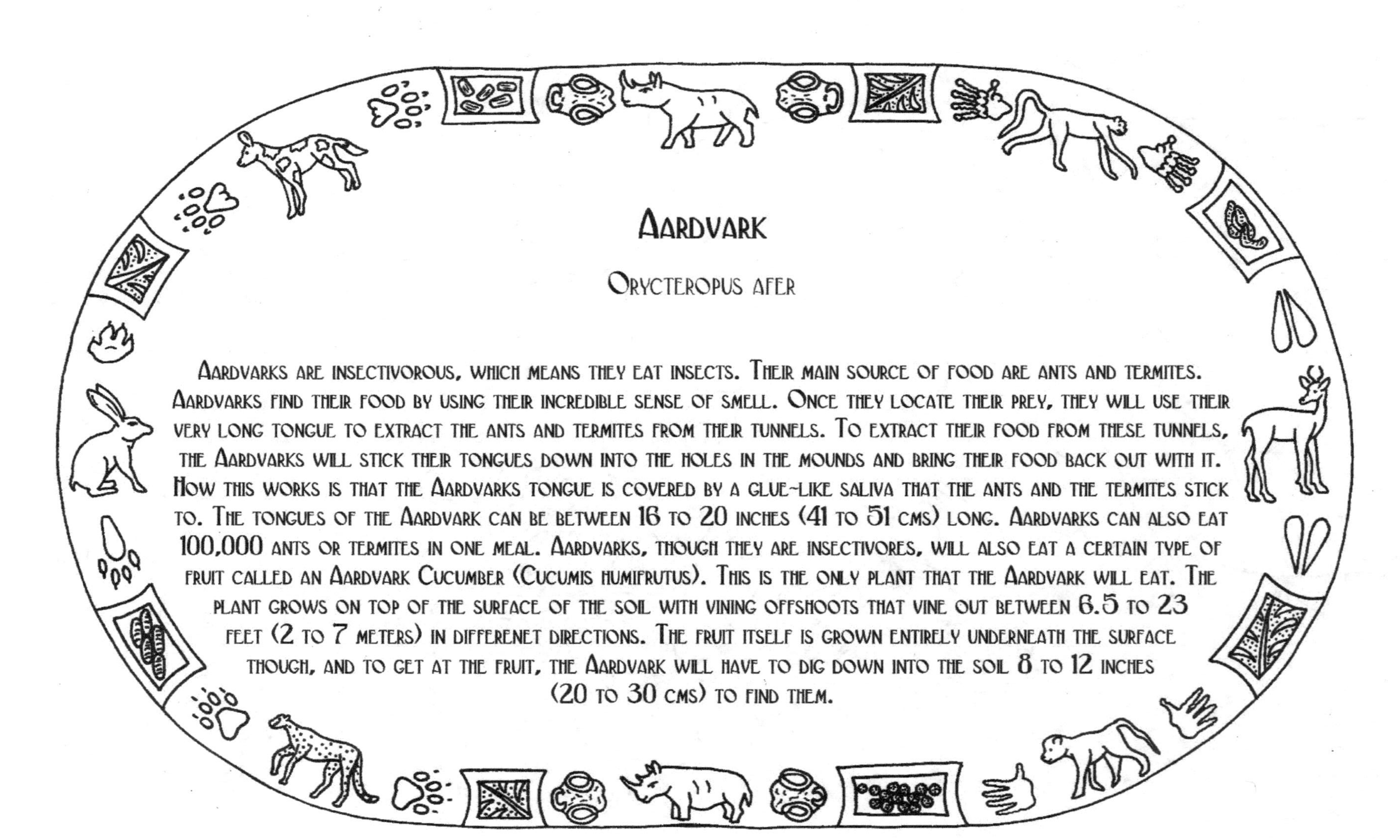

Aardvark

Orycteropus afer

Aardvarks are insectivorous, which means they eat insects. Their main source of food are ants and termites. Aardvarks find their food by using their incredible sense of smell. Once they locate their prey, they will use their very long tongue to extract the ants and termites from their tunnels. To extract their food from these tunnels, the Aardvarks will stick their tongues down into the holes in the mounds and bring their food back out with it. How this works is that the Aardvarks tongue is covered by a glue-like saliva that the ants and the termites stick to. The tongues of the Aardvark can be between 16 to 20 inches (41 to 51 cms) long. Aardvarks can also eat 100,000 ants or termites in one meal. Aardvarks, though they are insectivores, will also eat a certain type of fruit called an Aardvark Cucumber (Cucumis humifrutus). This is the only plant that the Aardvark will eat. The plant grows on top of the surface of the soil with vining offshoots that vine out between 6.5 to 23 feet (2 to 7 meters) in differenet directions. The fruit itself is grown entirely underneath the surface though, and to get at the fruit, the Aardvark will have to dig down into the soil 8 to 12 inches (20 to 30 cms) to find them.

Aardvark

Orycteropus afer

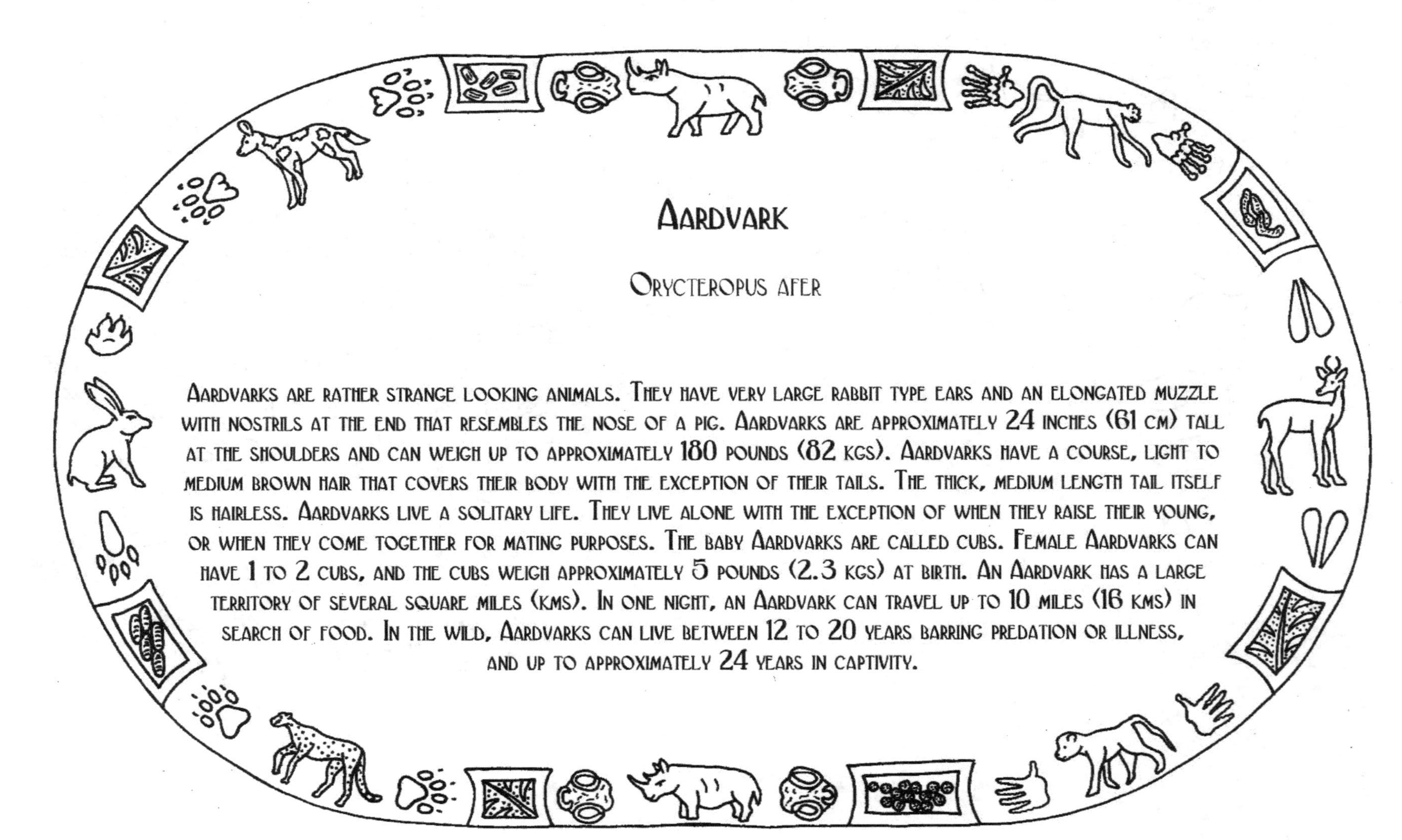

Aardvarks are rather strange looking animals. They have very large rabbit type ears and an elongated muzzle with nostrils at the end that resembles the nose of a pig. Aardvarks are approximately 24 inches (61 cm) tall at the shoulders and can weigh up to approximately 180 pounds (82 kgs). Aardvarks have a course, light to medium brown hair that covers their body with the exception of their tails. The thick, medium length tail itself is hairless. Aardvarks live a solitary life. They live alone with the exception of when they raise their young, or when they come together for mating purposes. The baby Aardvarks are called cubs. Female Aardvarks can have 1 to 2 cubs, and the cubs weigh approximately 5 pounds (2.3 kgs) at birth. An Aardvark has a large territory of several square miles (kms). In one night, an Aardvark can travel up to 10 miles (16 kms) in search of food. In the wild, Aardvarks can live between 12 to 20 years barring predation or illness, and up to approximately 24 years in captivity.

Black~Backed Jackal

Canis Mesomelas

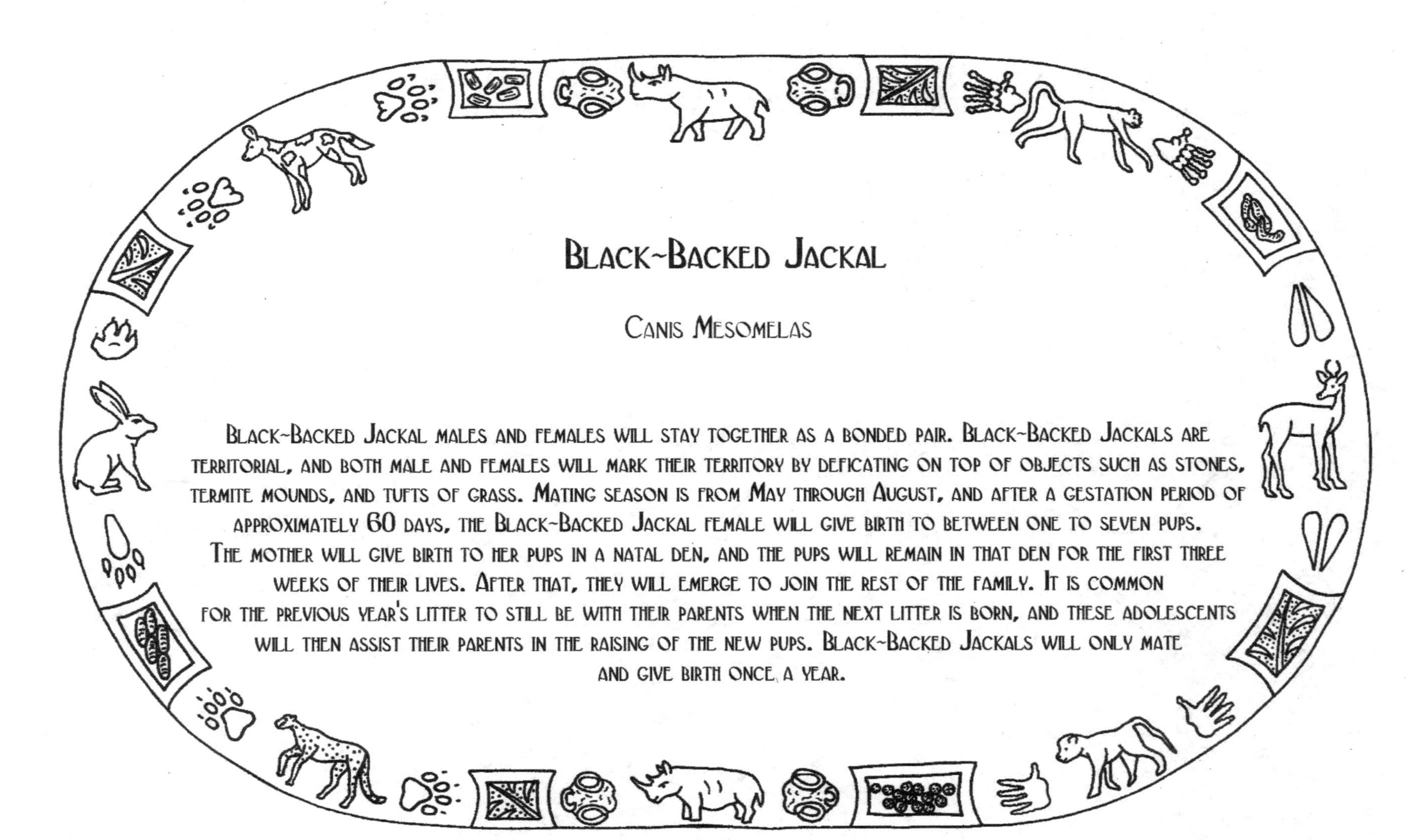

Black~Backed Jackal males and females will stay together as a bonded pair. Black~Backed Jackals are territorial, and both male and females will mark their territory by deficating on top of objects such as stones, termite mounds, and tufts of grass. Mating season is from May through August, and after a gestation period of approximately 60 days, the Black~Backed Jackal female will give birth to between one to seven pups.
The mother will give birth to her pups in a natal den, and the pups will remain in that den for the first three weeks of their lives. After that, they will emerge to join the rest of the family. It is common for the previous year's litter to still be with their parents when the next litter is born, and these adolescents will then assist their parents in the raising of the new pups. Black~Backed Jackals will only mate and give birth once, a year.

Black~Backed Jackal

Canis Mesomelas

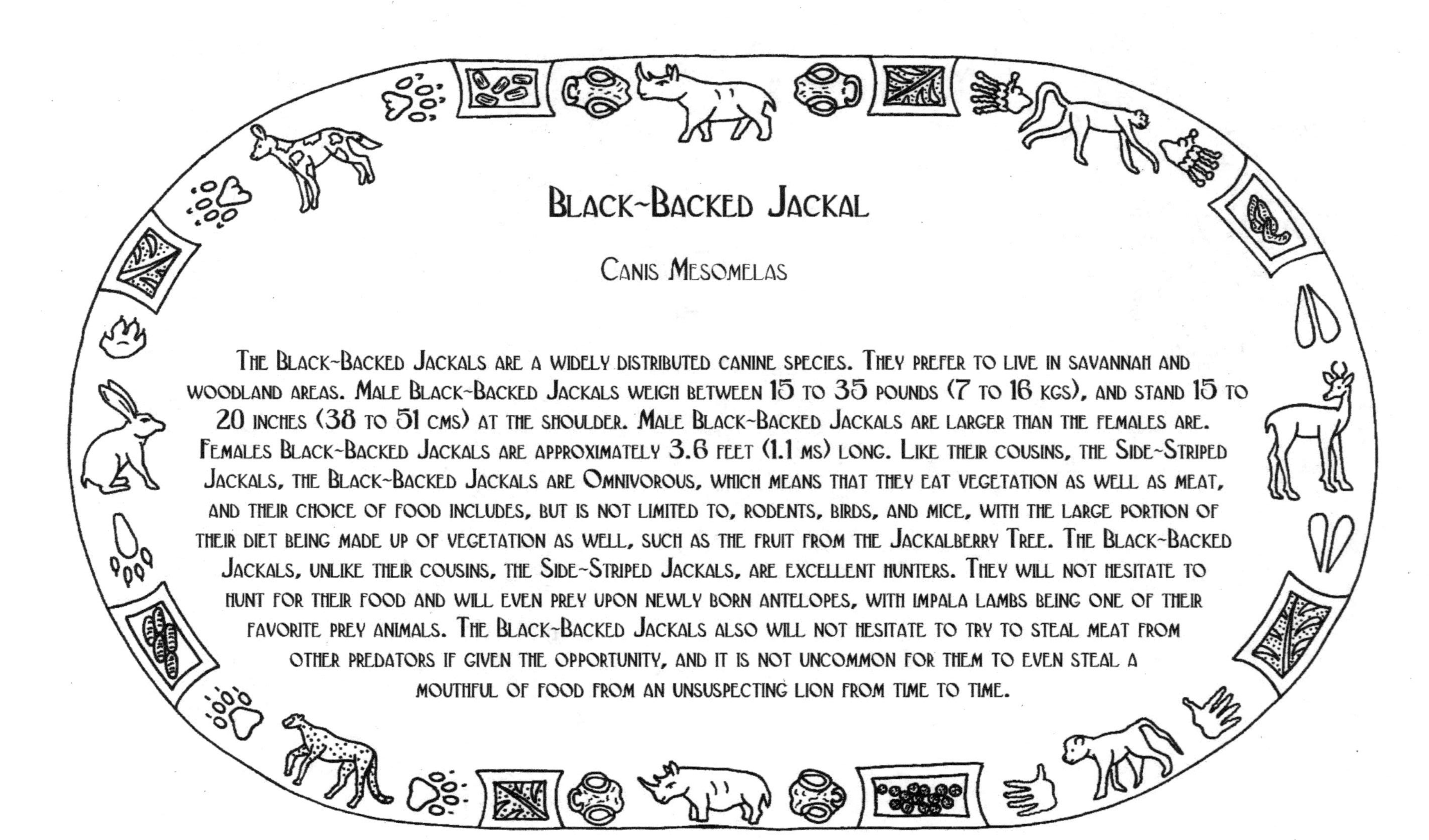

The Black~Backed Jackals are a widely distributed canine species. They prefer to live in savannah and woodland areas. Male Black~Backed Jackals weigh between 15 to 35 pounds (7 to 16 kgs), and stand 15 to 20 inches (38 to 51 cms) at the shoulder. Male Black~Backed Jackals are larger than the females are. Females Black~Backed Jackals are approximately 3.6 feet (1.1 ms) long. Like their cousins, the Side~Striped Jackals, the Black~Backed Jackals are Omnivorous, which means that they eat vegetation as well as meat, and their choice of food includes, but is not limited to, rodents, birds, and mice, with the large portion of their diet being made up of vegetation as well, such as the fruit from the Jackalberry Tree. The Black~Backed Jackals, unlike their cousins, the Side~Striped Jackals, are excellent hunters. They will not hesitate to hunt for their food and will even prey upon newly born antelopes, with impala lambs being one of their favorite prey animals. The Black~Backed Jackals also will not hesitate to try to steal meat from other predators if given the opportunity, and it is not uncommon for them to even steal a mouthful of food from an unsuspecting lion from time to time.

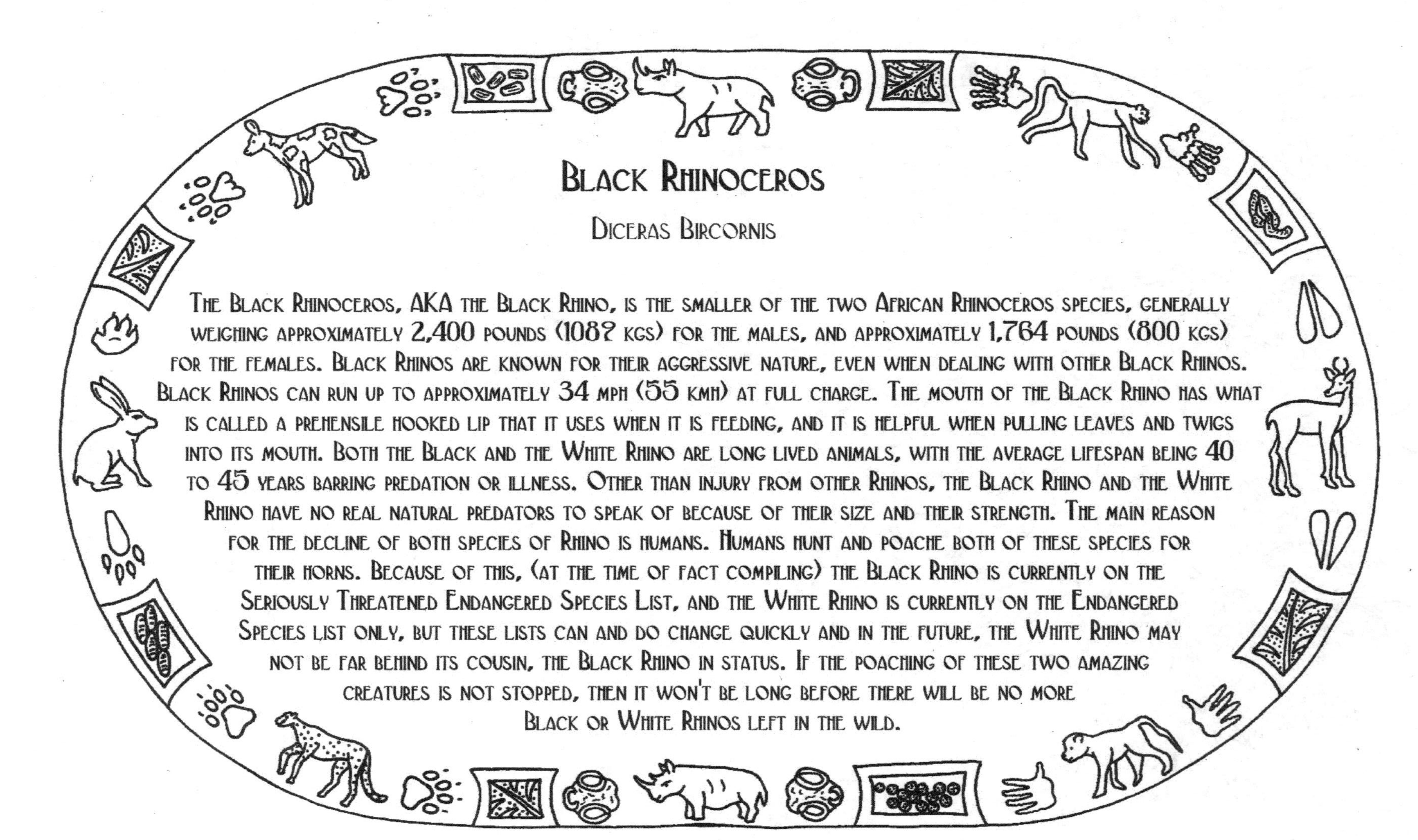

Black Rhinoceros

Diceras Bircornis

The Black Rhinoceros, AKA the Black Rhino, is the smaller of the two African Rhinoceros species, generally weighing approximately 2,400 pounds (1082 kgs) for the males, and approximately 1,764 pounds (800 kgs) for the females. Black Rhinos are known for their aggressive nature, even when dealing with other Black Rhinos. Black Rhinos can run up to approximately 34 mph (55 kmh) at full charge. The mouth of the Black Rhino has what is called a prehensile hooked lip that it uses when it is feeding, and it is helpful when pulling leaves and twigs into its mouth. Both the Black and the White Rhino are long lived animals, with the average lifespan being 40 to 45 years barring predation or illness. Other than injury from other Rhinos, the Black Rhino and the White Rhino have no real natural predators to speak of because of their size and their strength. The main reason for the decline of both species of Rhino is humans. Humans hunt and poache both of these species for their horns. Because of this, (at the time of fact compiling) the Black Rhino is currently on the Seriously Threatened Endangered Species List, and the White Rhino is currently on the Endangered Species list only, but these lists can and do change quickly and in the future, the White Rhino may not be far behind its cousin, the Black Rhino in status. If the poaching of these two amazing creatures is not stopped, then it won't be long before there will be no more Black or White Rhinos left in the wild.

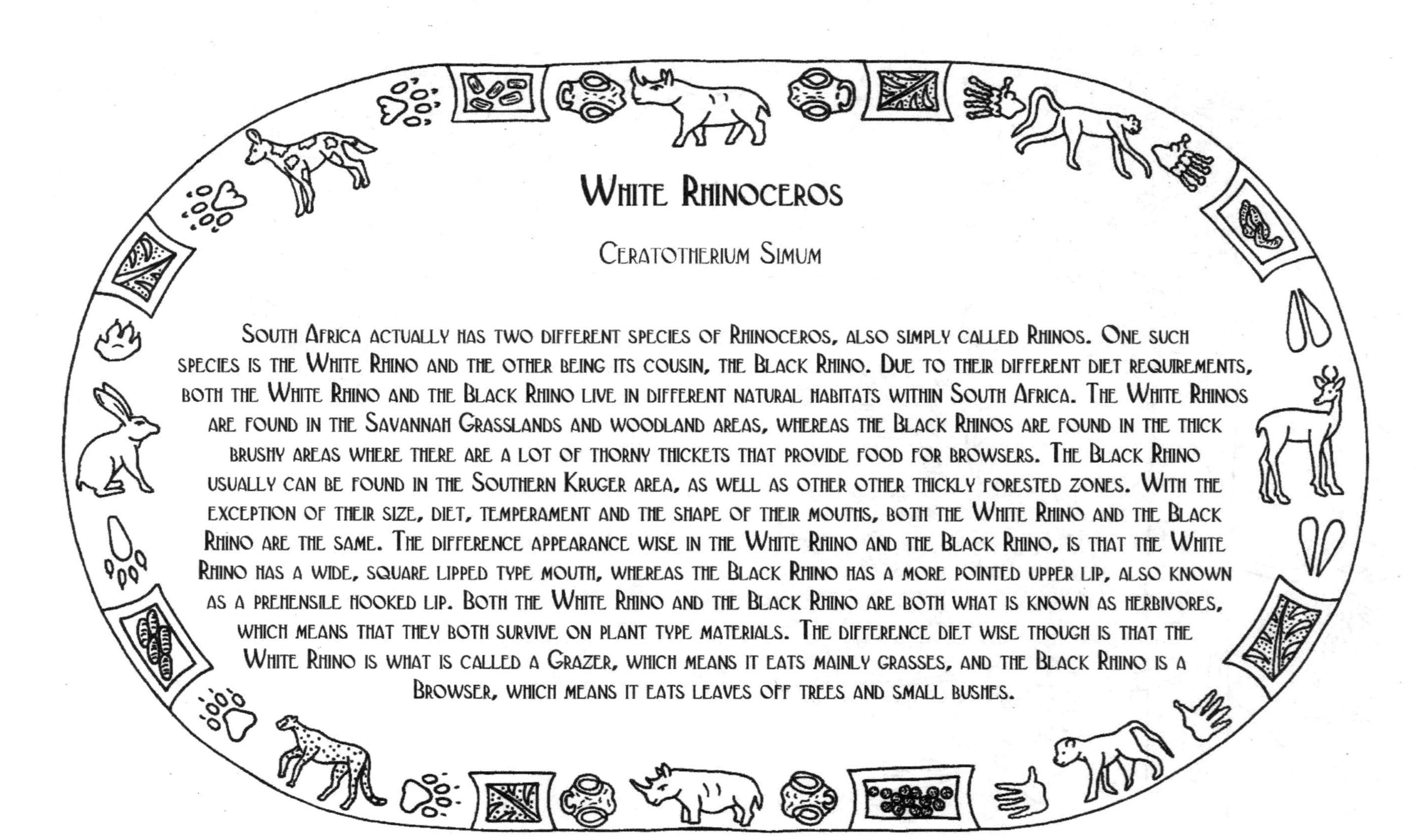

White Rhinoceros

Ceratotherium Simum

South Africa actually has two different species of Rhinoceros, also simply called Rhinos. One such species is the White Rhino and the other being its cousin, the Black Rhino. Due to their different diet requirements, both the White Rhino and the Black Rhino live in different natural habitats within South Africa. The White Rhinos are found in the Savannah Grasslands and woodland areas, whereas the Black Rhinos are found in the thick brushy areas where there are a lot of thorny thickets that provide food for browsers. The Black Rhino usually can be found in the Southern Kruger area, as well as other other thickly forested zones. With the exception of their size, diet, temperament and the shape of their mouths, both the White Rhino and the Black Rhino are the same. The difference appearance wise in the White Rhino and the Black Rhino, is that the White Rhino has a wide, square lipped type mouth, whereas the Black Rhino has a more pointed upper lip, also known as a prehensile hooked lip. Both the White Rhino and the Black Rhino are both what is known as herbivores, which means that they both survive on plant type materials. The difference diet wise though is that the White Rhino is what is called a Grazer, which means it eats mainly grasses, and the Black Rhino is a Browser, which means it eats leaves off trees and small bushes.

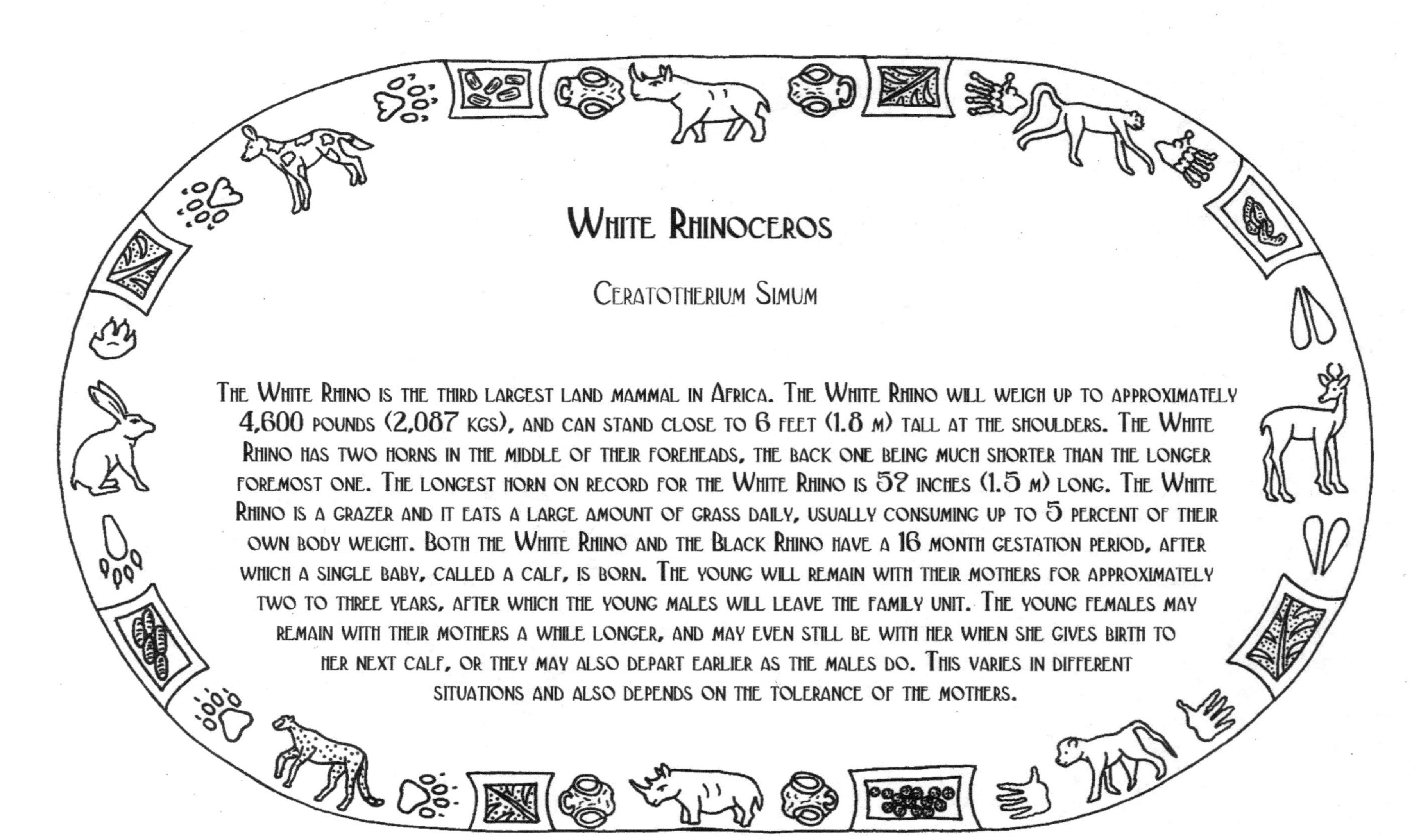

White Rhinoceros

Ceratotherium Simum

The White Rhino is the third largest land mammal in Africa. The White Rhino will weigh up to approximately 4,600 pounds (2,087 kgs), and can stand close to 6 feet (1.8 m) tall at the shoulders. The White Rhino has two horns in the middle of their foreheads, the back one being much shorter than the longer foremost one. The longest horn on record for the White Rhino is 52 inches (1.5 m) long. The White Rhino is a grazer and it eats a large amount of grass daily, usually consuming up to 5 percent of their own body weight. Both the White Rhino and the Black Rhino have a 16 month gestation period, after which a single baby, called a calf, is born. The young will remain with their mothers for approximately two to three years, after which the young males will leave the family unit. The young females may remain with their mothers a while longer, and may even still be with her when she gives birth to her next calf, or they may also depart earlier as the males do. This varies in different situations and also depends on the tolerance of the mothers.

Bushbuck

Tragelphus Scriptus

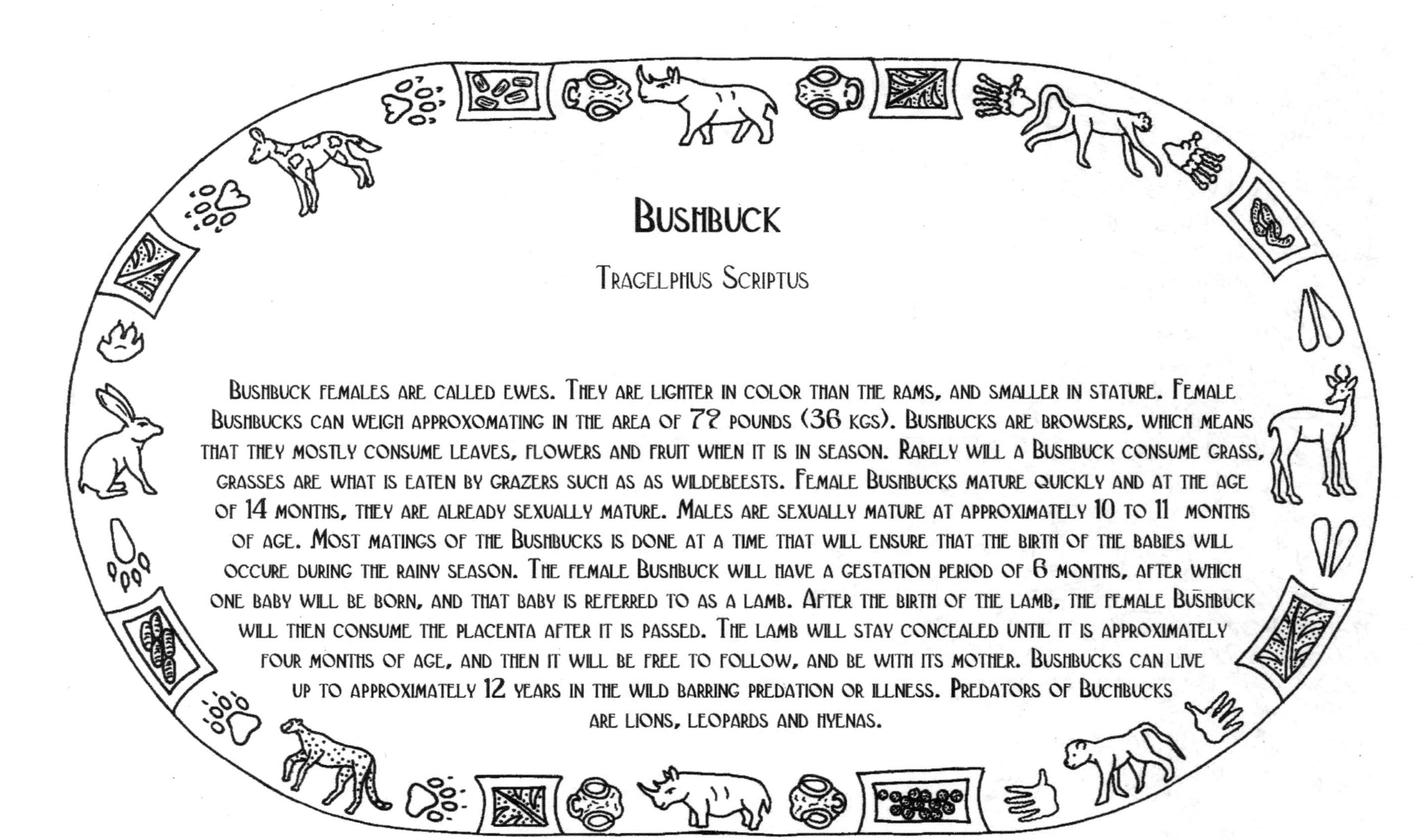

Bushbuck females are called ewes. They are lighter in color than the rams, and smaller in stature. Female Bushbucks can weigh approxomating in the area of 72 pounds (36 kgs). Bushbucks are browsers, which means that they mostly consume leaves, flowers and fruit when it is in season. Rarely will a Bushbuck consume grass, grasses are what is eaten by grazers such as as wildebeests. Female Bushbucks mature quickly and at the age of 14 months, they are already sexually mature. Males are sexually mature at approximately 10 to 11 months of age. Most matings of the Bushbucks is done at a time that will ensure that the birth of the babies will occure during the rainy season. The female Bushbuck will have a gestation period of 6 months, after which one baby will be born, and that baby is referred to as a lamb. After the birth of the lamb, the female Bushbuck will then consume the placenta after it is passed. The lamb will stay concealed until it is approximately four months of age, and then it will be free to follow, and be with its mother. Bushbucks can live up to approximately 12 years in the wild barring predation or illness. Predators of Buchbucks are lions, leopards and hyenas.

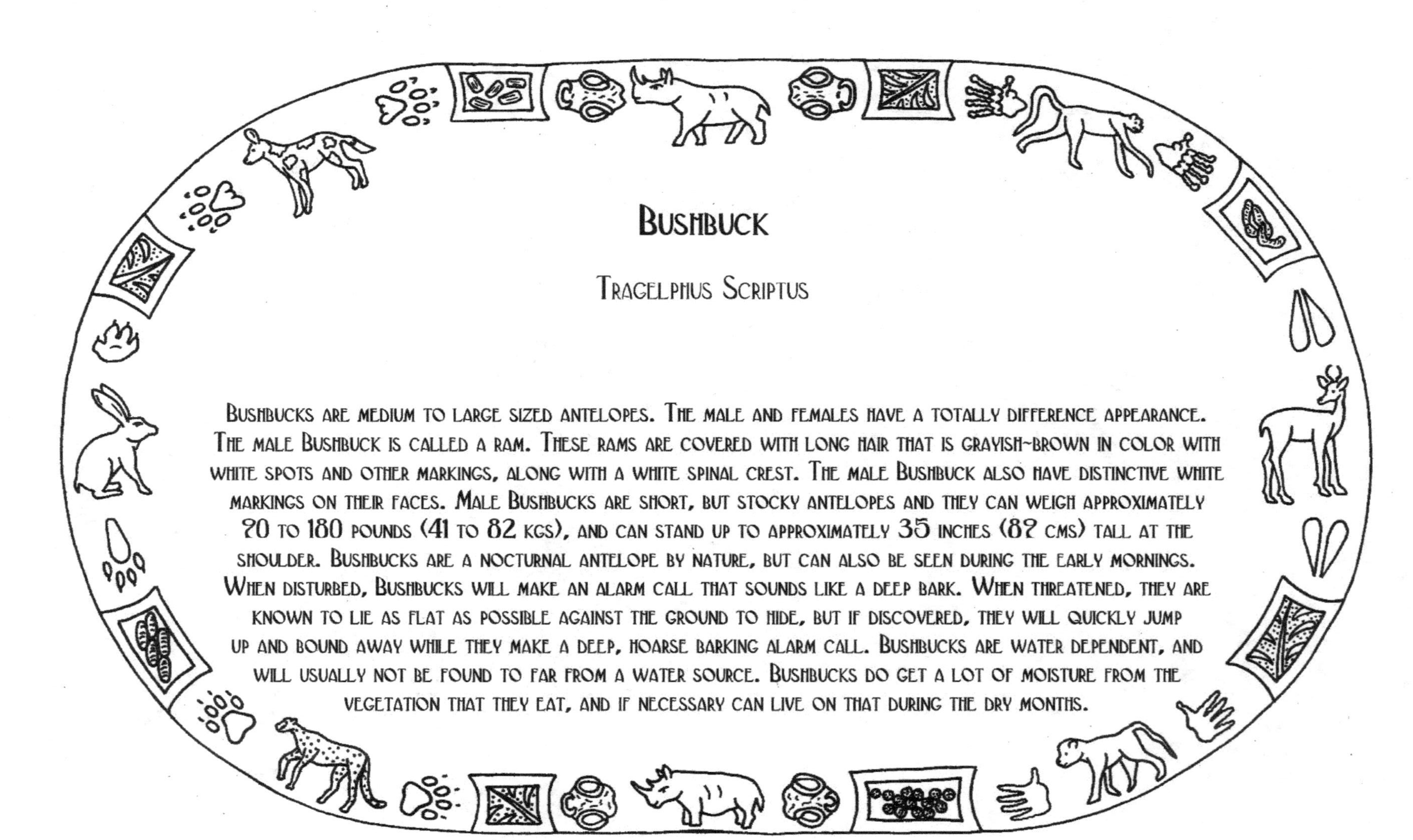

Bushbuck

Tragelphus Scriptus

Bushbucks are medium to large sized antelopes. The male and females have a totally difference appearance. The male Bushbuck is called a ram. These rams are covered with long hair that is grayish~brown in color with white spots and other markings, along with a white spinal crest. The male Bushbuck also have distinctive white markings on their faces. Male Bushbucks are short, but stocky antelopes and they can weigh approximately 20 to 180 pounds (41 to 82 kgs), and can stand up to approximately 35 inches (82 cms) tall at the shoulder. Bushbucks are a nocturnal antelope by nature, but can also be seen during the early mornings. When disturbed, Bushbucks will make an alarm call that sounds like a deep bark. When threatened, they are known to lie as flat as possible against the ground to hide, but if discovered, they will quickly jump up and bound away while they make a deep, hoarse barking alarm call. Bushbucks are water dependent, and will usually not be found to far from a water source. Bushbucks do get a lot of moisture from the vegetation that they eat, and if necessary can live on that during the dry months.

Chacma Baboon

Papio Ursinus

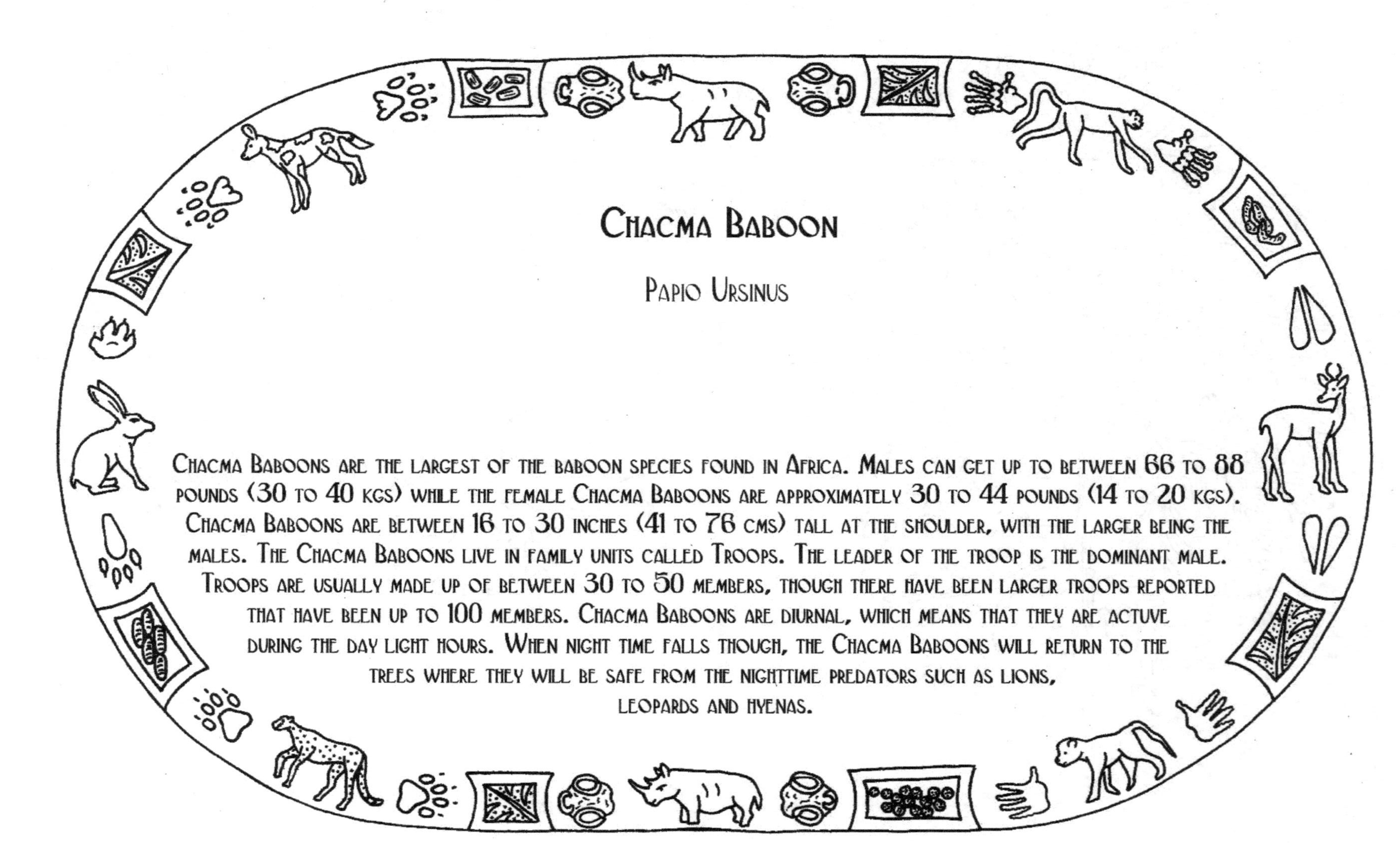

Chacma Baboons are the largest of the baboon species found in Africa. Males can get up to between 66 to 88 pounds (30 to 40 kgs) while the female Chacma Baboons are approximately 30 to 44 pounds (14 to 20 kgs). Chacma Baboons are between 16 to 30 inches (41 to 76 cms) tall at the shoulder, with the larger being the males. The Chacma Baboons live in family units called Troops. The leader of the troop is the dominant male. Troops are usually made up of between 30 to 50 members, though there have been larger troops reported that have been up to 100 members. Chacma Baboons are diurnal, which means that they are actuve during the day light hours. When night time falls though, the Chacma Baboons will return to the trees where they will be safe from the nighttime predators such as lions, leopards and hyenas.

Chacma Baboon

Papio Ursinus

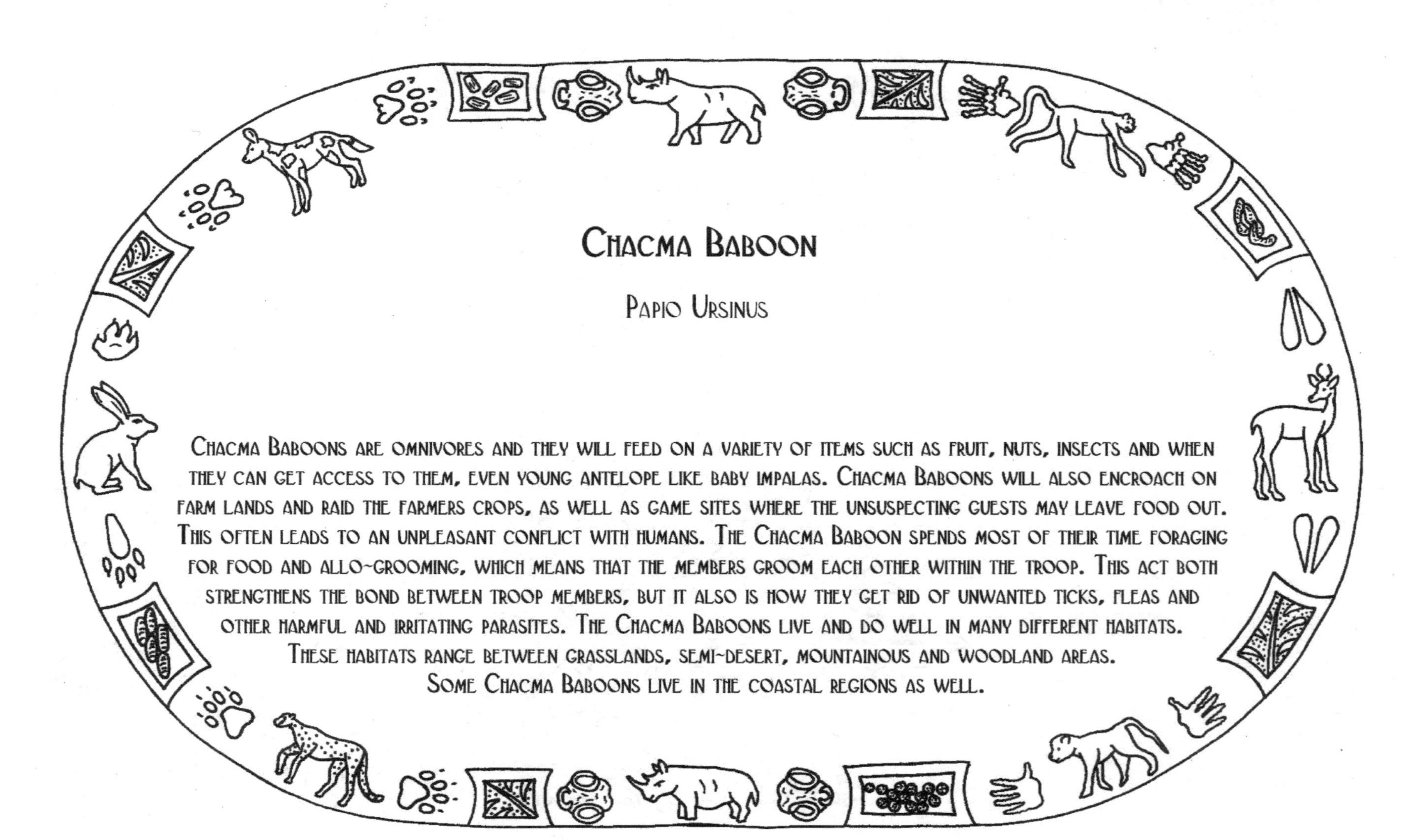

Chacma Baboons are omnivores and they will feed on a variety of items such as fruit, nuts, insects and when they can get access to them, even young antelope like baby impalas. Chacma Baboons will also encroach on farm lands and raid the farmers crops, as well as game sites where the unsuspecting guests may leave food out. This often leads to an unpleasant conflict with humans. The Chacma Baboon spends most of their time foraging for food and allo-grooming, which means that the members groom each other within the troop. This act both strengthens the bond between troop members, but it also is how they get rid of unwanted ticks, fleas and other harmful and irritating parasites. The Chacma Baboons live and do well in many different habitats. These habitats range between grasslands, semi-desert, mountainous and woodland areas. Some Chacma Baboons live in the coastal regions as well.

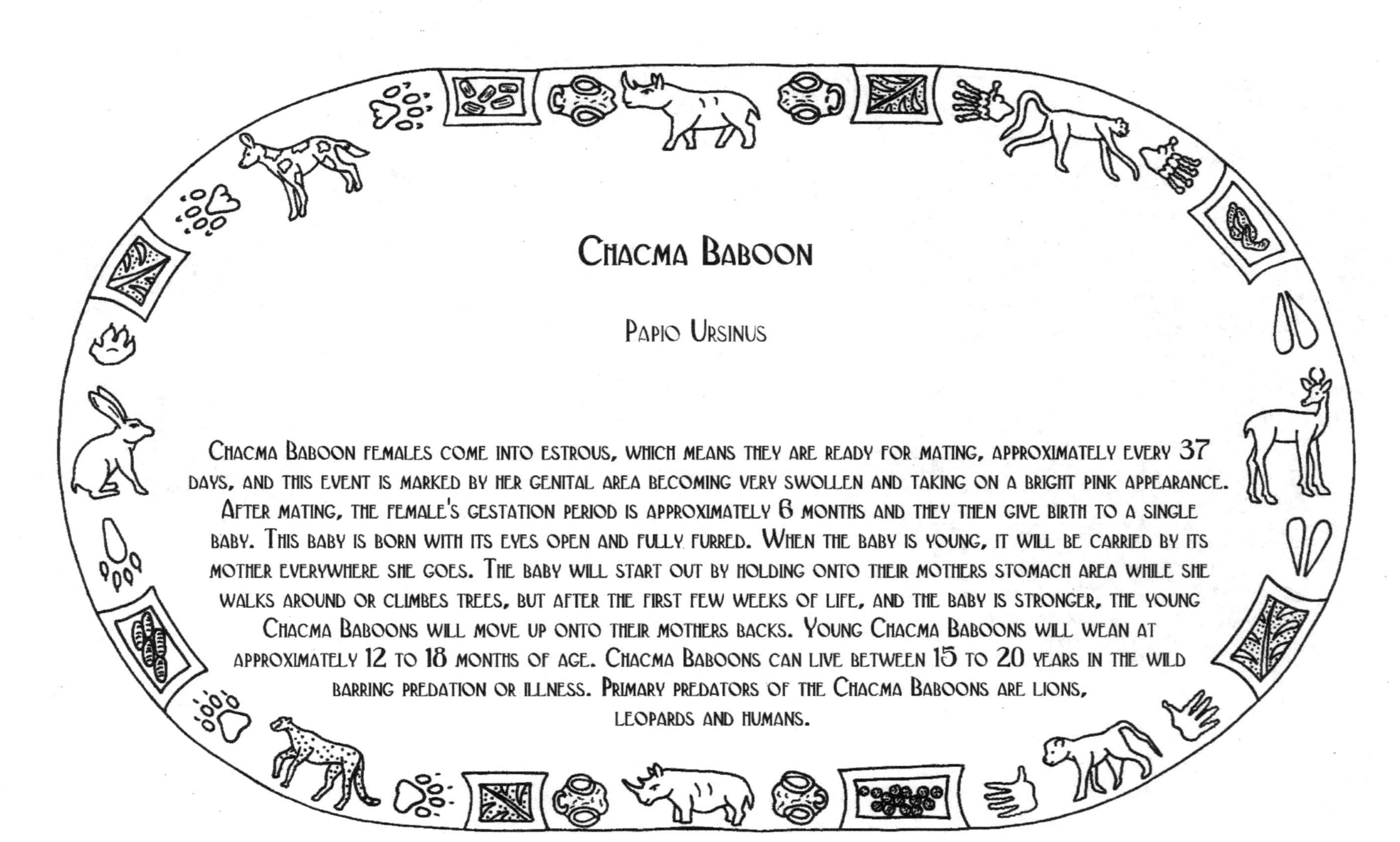

Chacma Baboon

Papio Ursinus

Chacma Baboon females come into estrous, which means they are ready for mating, approximately every 37 days, and this event is marked by her genital area becoming very swollen and taking on a bright pink appearance. After mating, the female's gestation period is approximately 6 months and they then give birth to a single baby. This baby is born with its eyes open and fully furred. When the baby is young, it will be carried by its mother everywhere she goes. The baby will start out by holding onto their mothers stomach area while she walks around or climbes trees, but after the first few weeks of life, and the baby is stronger, the young Chacma Baboons will move up onto their mothers backs. Young Chacma Baboons will wean at approximately 12 to 18 months of age. Chacma Baboons can live between 15 to 20 years in the wild barring predation or illness. Primary predators of the Chacma Baboons are lions, leopards and humans.

Cheetah

Acinocyx jubatus

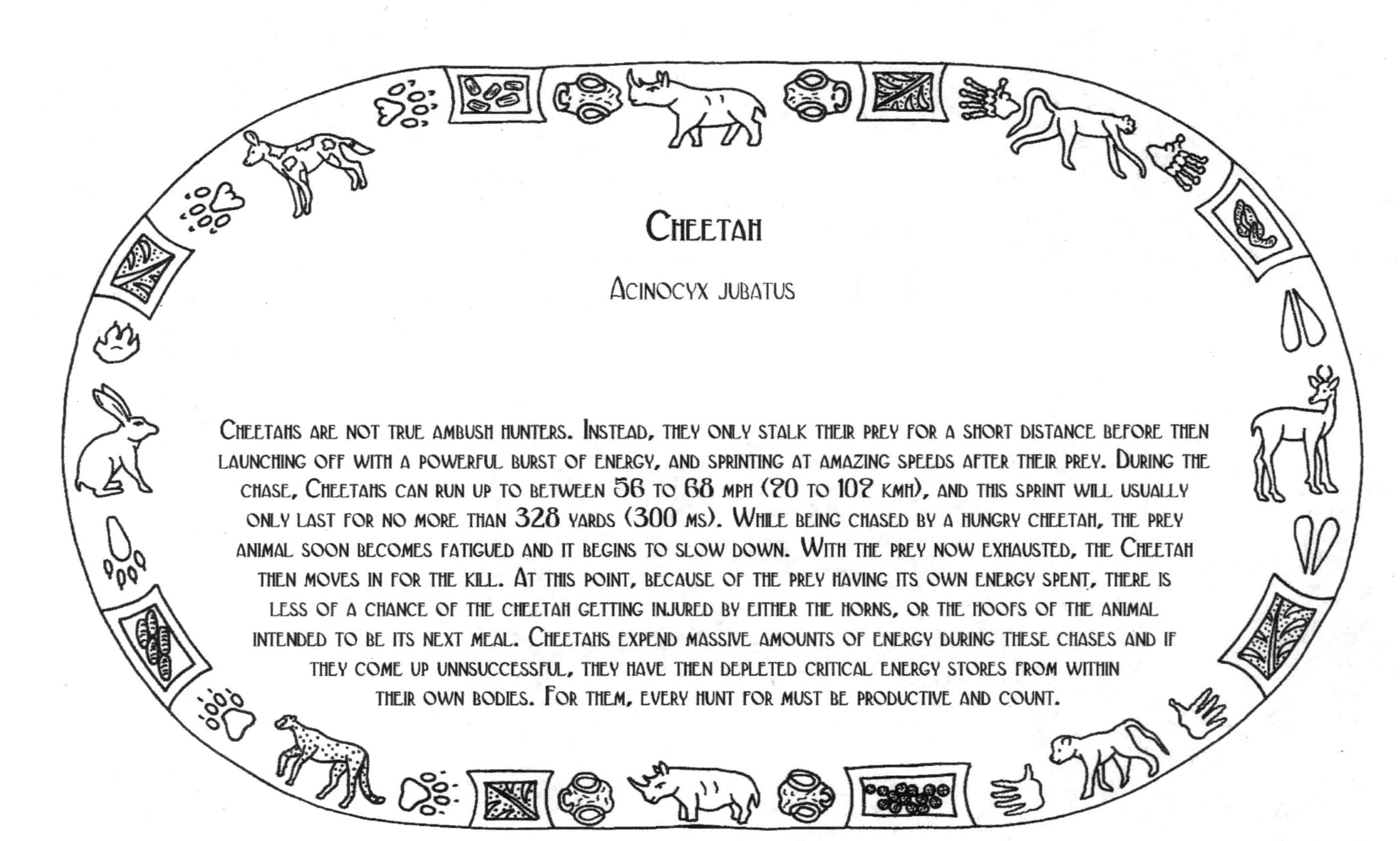

Cheetahs are not true ambush hunters. Instead, they only stalk their prey for a short distance before then launching off with a powerful burst of energy, and sprinting at amazing speeds after their prey. During the chase, Cheetahs can run up to between 56 to 68 mph (20 to 102 kmh), and this sprint will usually only last for no more than 328 yards (300 ms). While being chased by a hungry cheetah, the prey animal soon becomes fatigued and it begins to slow down. With the prey now exhausted, the Cheetah then moves in for the kill. At this point, because of the prey having its own energy spent, there is less of a chance of the cheetah getting injured by either the horns, or the hoofs of the animal intended to be its next meal. Cheetahs expend massive amounts of energy during these chases and if they come up unnsuccessful, they have then depleted critical energy stores from within their own bodies. For them, every hunt for must be productive and count.

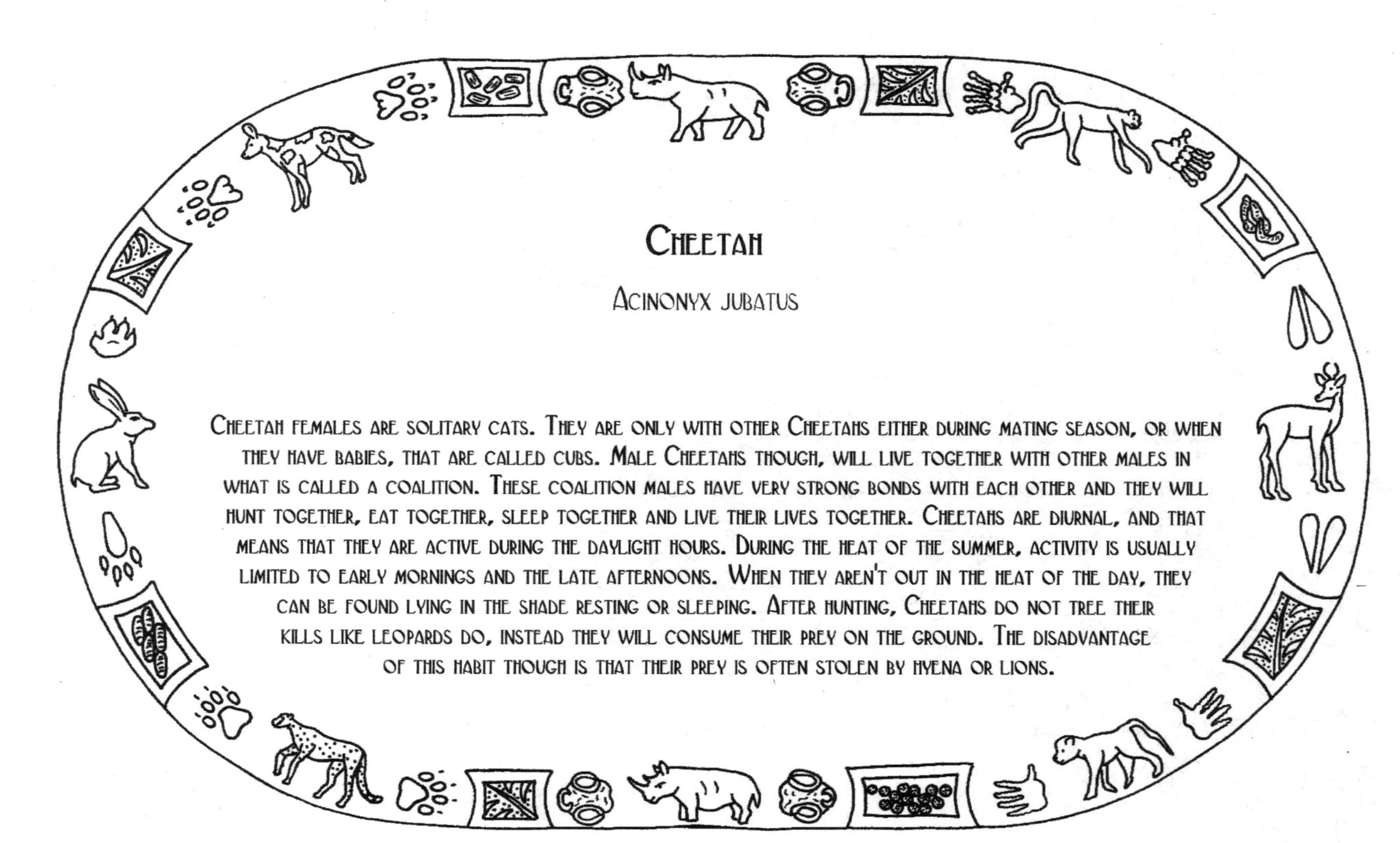

Cheetah

Acinonyx jubatus

Cheetah females are solitary cats. They are only with other Cheetahs either during mating season, or when they have babies, that are called cubs. Male Cheetahs though, will live together with other males in what is called a coalition. These coalition males have very strong bonds with each other and they will hunt together, eat together, sleep together and live their lives together. Cheetahs are diurnal, and that means that they are active during the daylight hours. During the heat of the summer, activity is usually limited to early mornings and the late afternoons. When they aren't out in the heat of the day, they can be found lying in the shade resting or sleeping. After hunting, Cheetahs do not tree their kills like leopards do, instead they will consume their prey on the ground. The disadvantage of this habit though is that their prey is often stolen by hyena or lions.

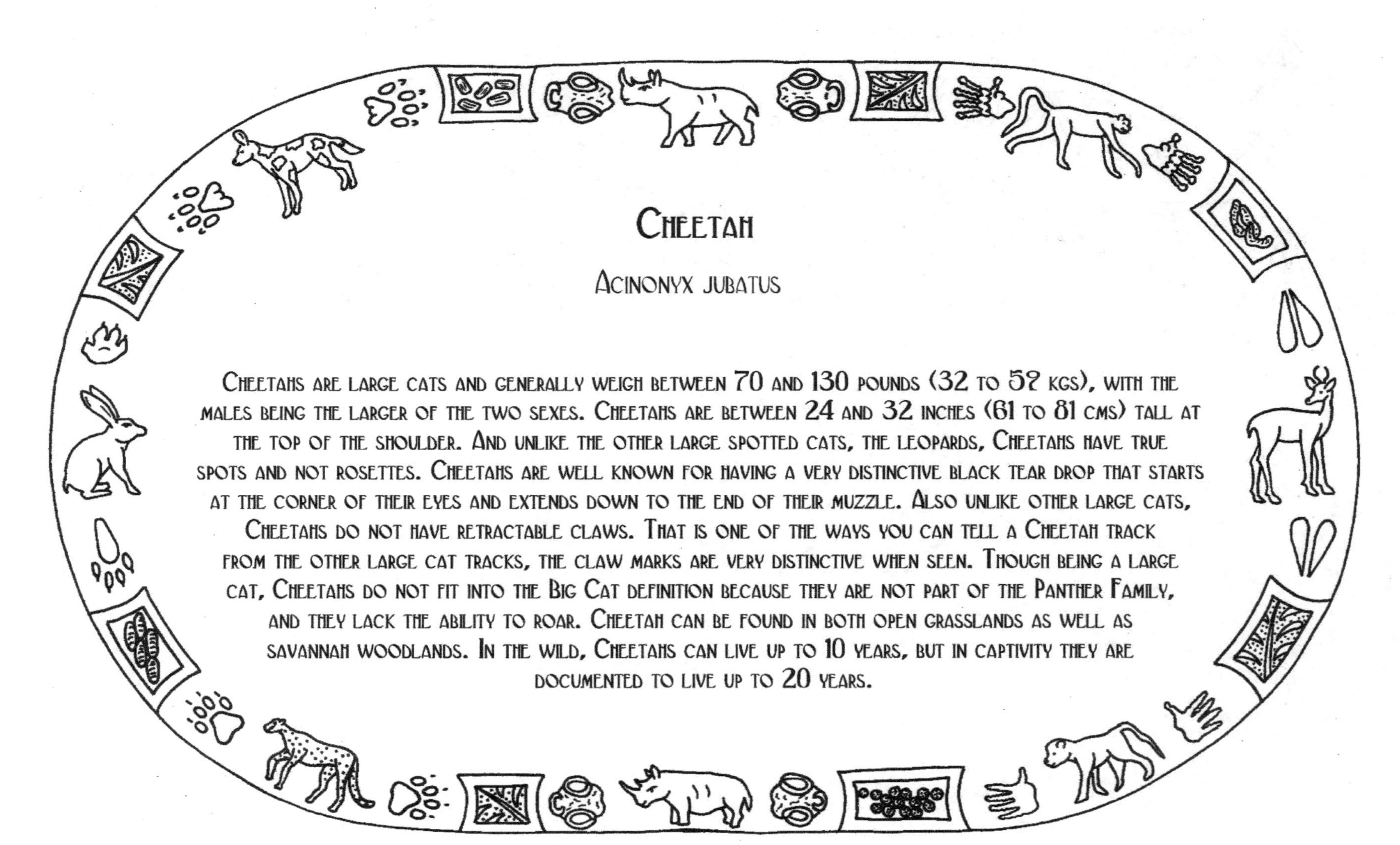

Cheetah

Acinonyx jubatus

Cheetahs are large cats and generally weigh between 70 and 130 pounds (32 to 58 kgs), with the males being the larger of the two sexes. Cheetahs are between 24 and 32 inches (61 to 81 cms) tall at the top of the shoulder. And unlike the other large spotted cats, the leopards, Cheetahs have true spots and not rosettes. Cheetahs are well known for having a very distinctive black tear drop that starts at the corner of their eyes and extends down to the end of their muzzle. Also unlike other large cats, Cheetahs do not have retractable claws. That is one of the ways you can tell a Cheetah track from the other large cat tracks, the claw marks are very distinctive when seen. Though being a large cat, Cheetahs do not fit into the Big Cat definition because they are not part of the Panther Family, and they lack the ability to roar. Cheetah can be found in both open grasslands as well as savannah woodlands. In the wild, Cheetahs can live up to 10 years, but in captivity they are documented to live up to 20 years.

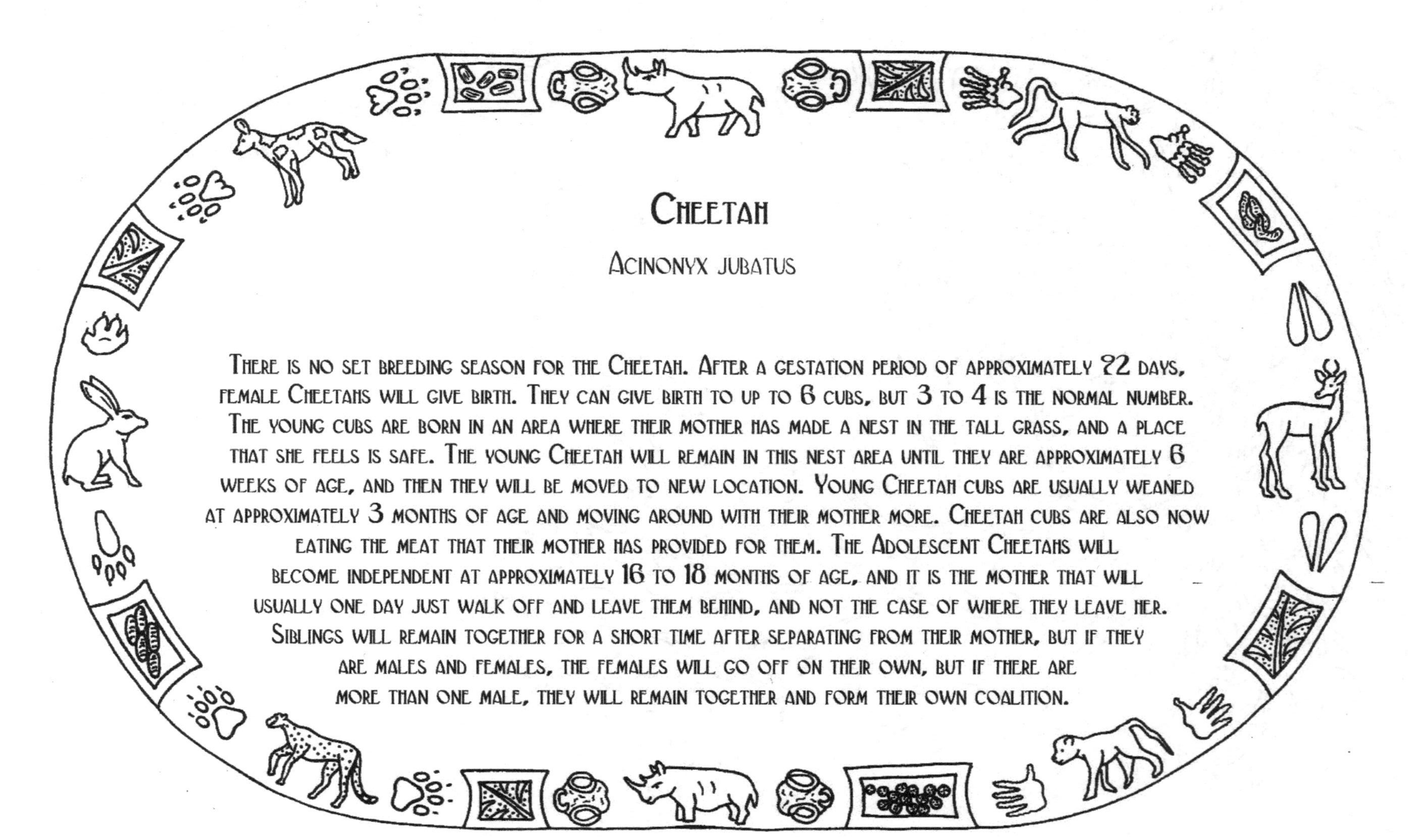

Cheetah

Acinonyx jubatus

There is no set breeding season for the Cheetah. After a gestation period of approximately 22 days, female Cheetahs will give birth. They can give birth to up to 6 cubs, but 3 to 4 is the normal number. The young cubs are born in an area where their mother has made a nest in the tall grass, and a place that she feels is safe. The young Cheetah will remain in this nest area until they are approximately 6 weeks of age, and then they will be moved to new location. Young Cheetah cubs are usually weaned at approximately 3 months of age and moving around with their mother more. Cheetah cubs are also now eating the meat that their mother has provided for them. The Adolescent Cheetahs will become independent at approximately 16 to 18 months of age, and it is the mother that will usually one day just walk off and leave them behind, and not the case of where they leave her. Siblings will remain together for a short time after separating from their mother, but if they are males and females, the females will go off on their own, but if there are more than one male, they will remain together and form their own coalition.

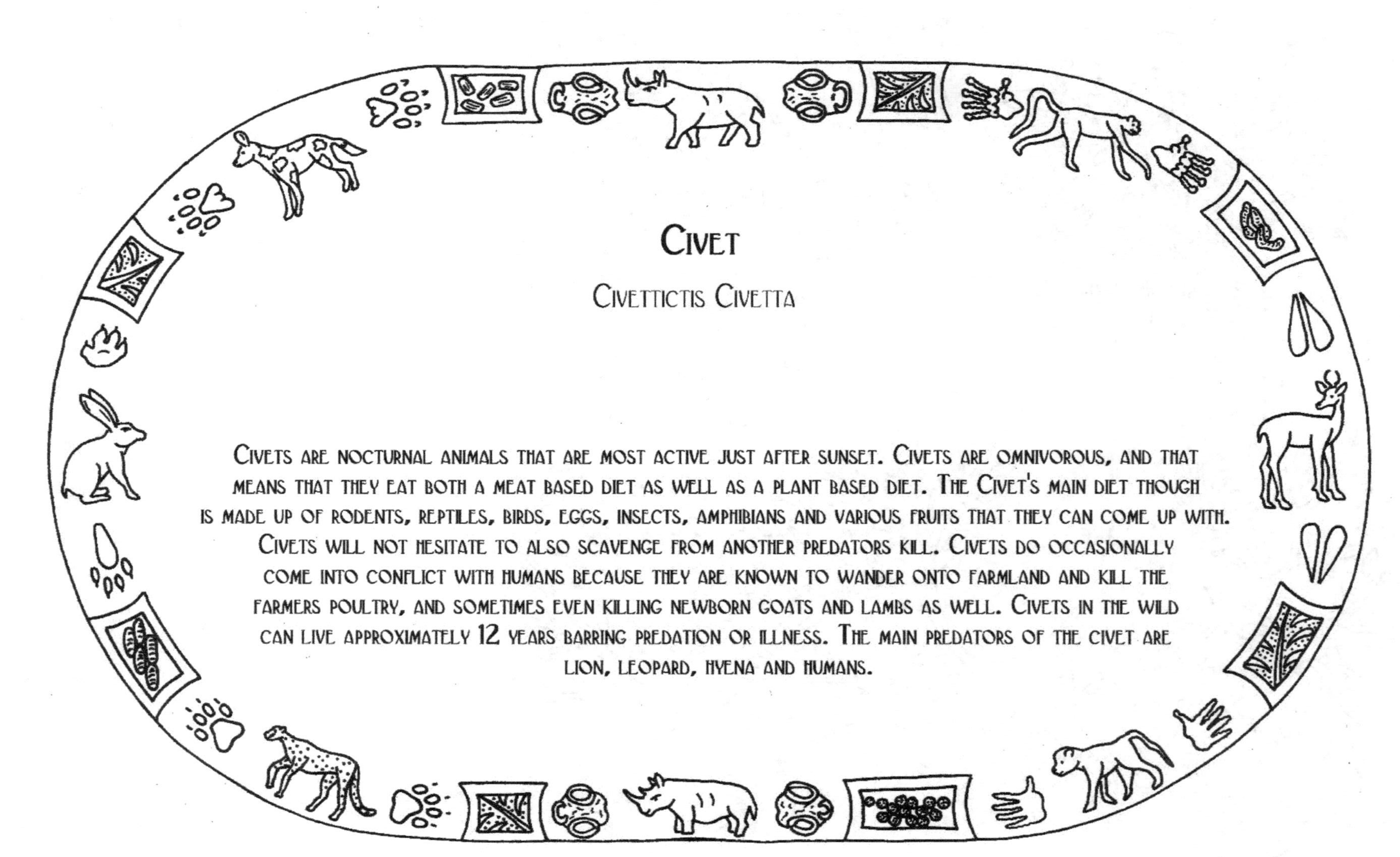

Civet

Civettictis Civetta

Civets are nocturnal animals that are most active just after sunset. Civets are omnivorous, and that means that they eat both a meat based diet as well as a plant based diet. The Civet's main diet though is made up of rodents, reptiles, birds, eggs, insects, amphibians and various fruits that they can come up with. Civets will not hesitate to also scavenge from another predators kill. Civets do occasionally come into conflict with humans because they are known to wander onto farmland and kill the farmers poultry, and sometimes even killing newborn goats and lambs as well. Civets in the wild can live approximately 12 years barring predation or illness. The main predators of the civet are lion, leopard, hyena and humans.

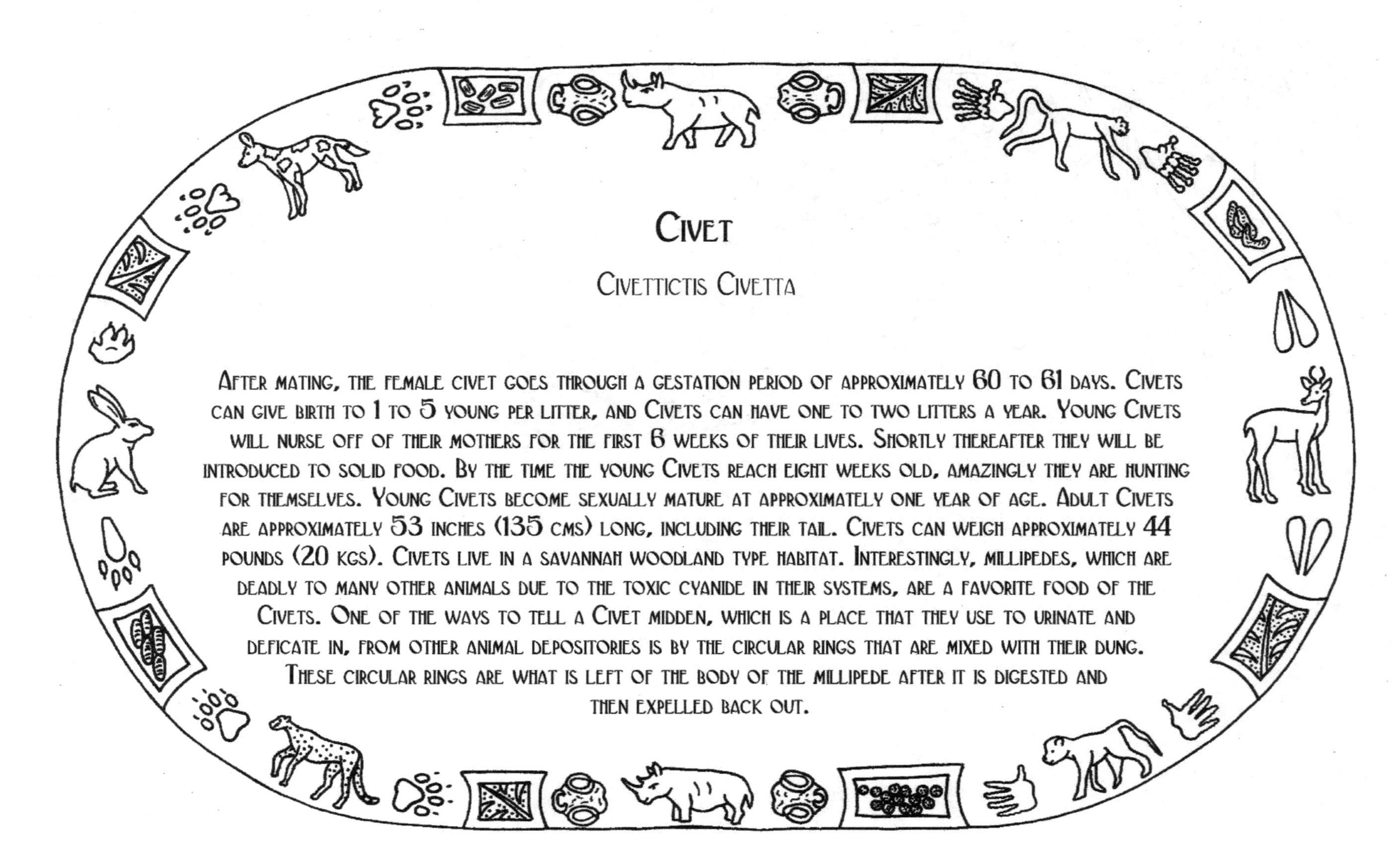

Civet

Civettictis Civetta

After mating, the female civet goes through a gestation period of approximately 60 to 61 days. Civets can give birth to 1 to 5 young per litter, and Civets can have one to two litters a year. Young Civets will nurse off of their mothers for the first 6 weeks of their lives. Shortly thereafter they will be introduced to solid food. By the time the young Civets reach eight weeks old, amazingly they are hunting for themselves. Young Civets become sexually mature at approximately one year of age. Adult Civets are approximately 53 inches (135 cms) long, including their tail. Civets can weigh approximately 44 pounds (20 kgs). Civets live in a savannah woodland type habitat. Interestingly, millipedes, which are deadly to many other animals due to the toxic cyanide in their systems, are a favorite food of the Civets. One of the ways to tell a Civet midden, which is a place that they use to urinate and deficate in, from other animal depositories is by the circular rings that are mixed with their dung. These circular rings are what is left of the body of the millipede after it is digested and then expelled back out.

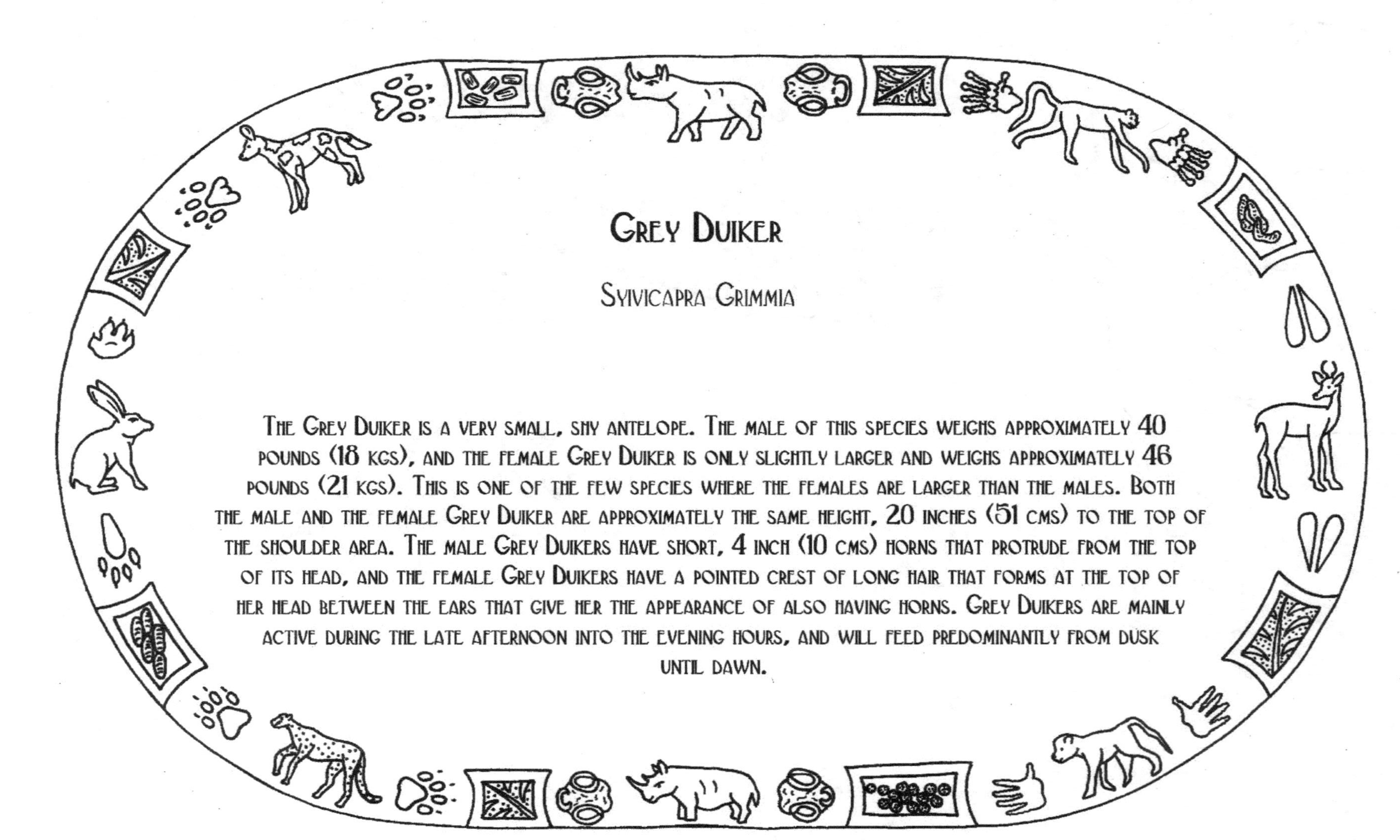

Grey Duiker

Sylvicapra Grimmia

The Grey Duiker is a very small, shy antelope. The male of this species weighs approximately 40 pounds (18 kgs), and the female Grey Duiker is only slightly larger and weighs approximately 46 pounds (21 kgs). This is one of the few species where the females are larger than the males. Both the male and the female Grey Duiker are approximately the same height, 20 inches (51 cms) to the top of the shoulder area. The male Grey Duikers have short, 4 inch (10 cms) horns that protrude from the top of its head, and the female Grey Duikers have a pointed crest of long hair that forms at the top of her head between the ears that give her the appearance of also having horns. Grey Duikers are mainly active during the late afternoon into the evening hours, and will feed predominantly from dusk until dawn.

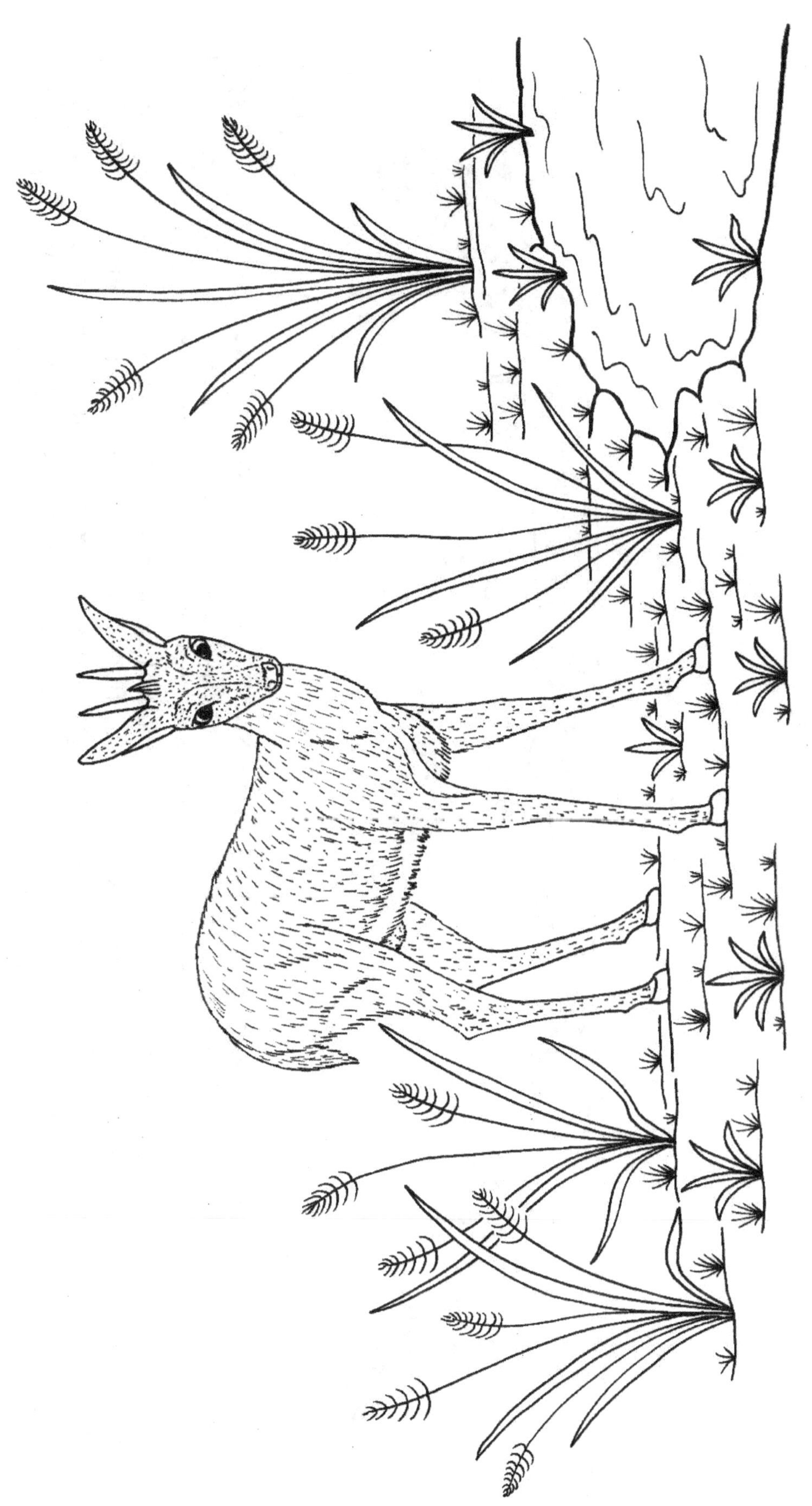

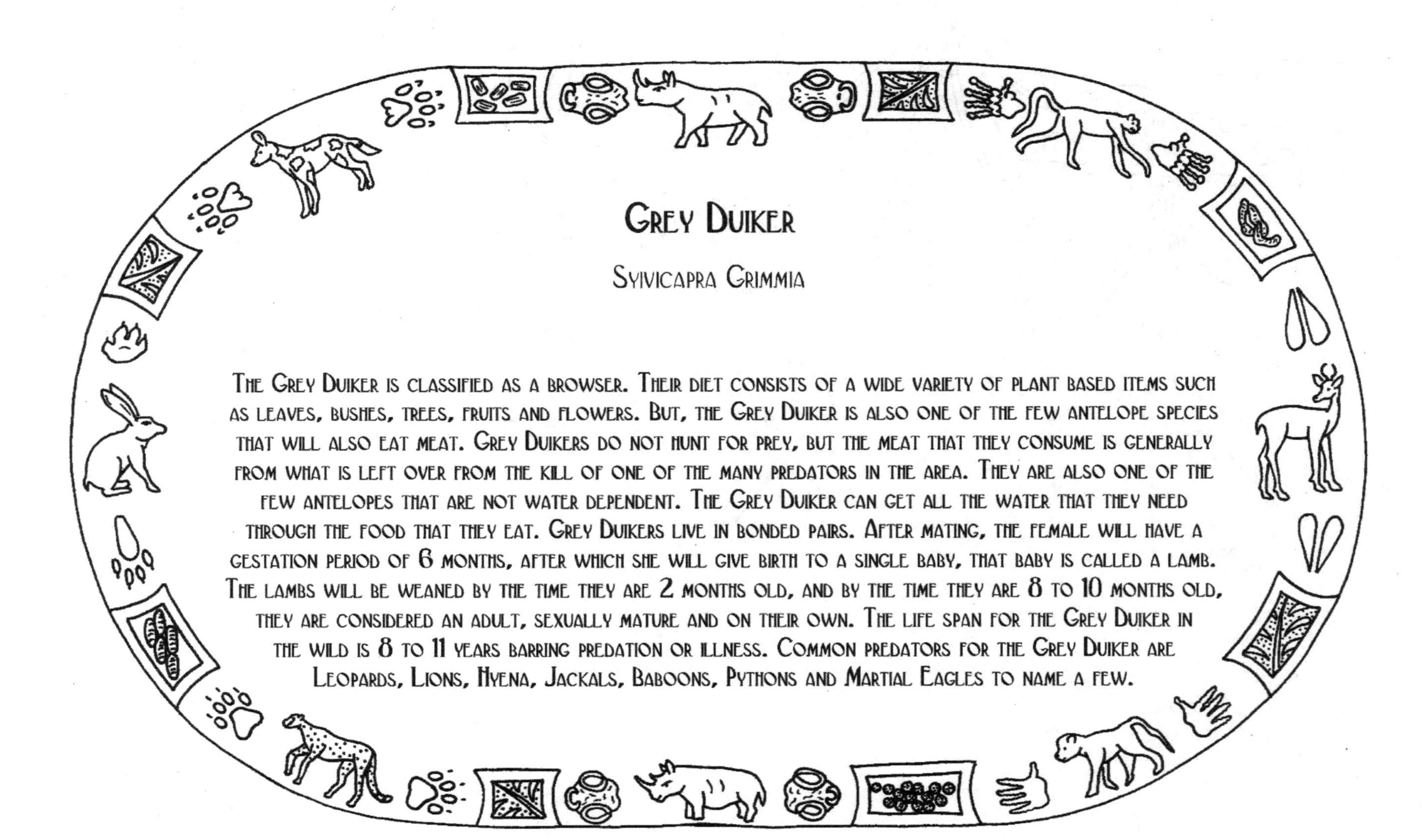

Grey Duiker

Syivicapra Grimmia

The Grey Duiker is classified as a browser. Their diet consists of a wide variety of plant based items such as leaves, bushes, trees, fruits and flowers. But, the Grey Duiker is also one of the few antelope species that will also eat meat. Grey Duikers do not hunt for prey, but the meat that they consume is generally from what is left over from the kill of one of the many predators in the area. They are also one of the few antelopes that are not water dependent. The Grey Duiker can get all the water that they need through the food that they eat. Grey Duikers live in bonded pairs. After mating, the female will have a gestation period of 6 months, after which she will give birth to a single baby, that baby is called a lamb. The lambs will be weaned by the time they are 2 months old, and by the time they are 8 to 10 months old, they are considered an adult, sexually mature and on their own. The life span for the Grey Duiker in the wild is 8 to 11 years barring predation or illness. Common predators for the Grey Duiker are Leopards, Lions, Hyena, Jackals, Baboons, Pythons and Martial Eagles to name a few.

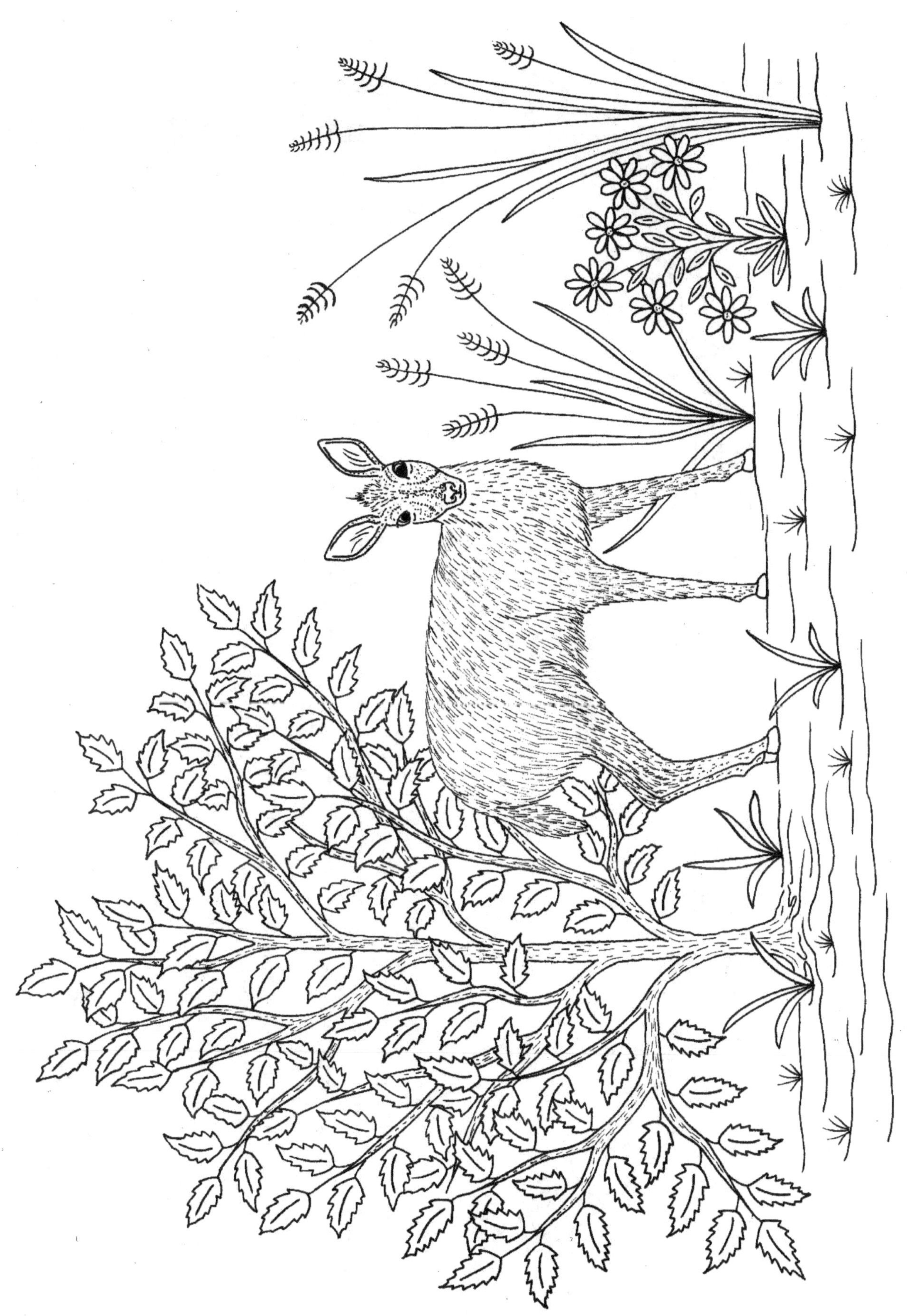

Ground Pangolin

Manis Temminckii

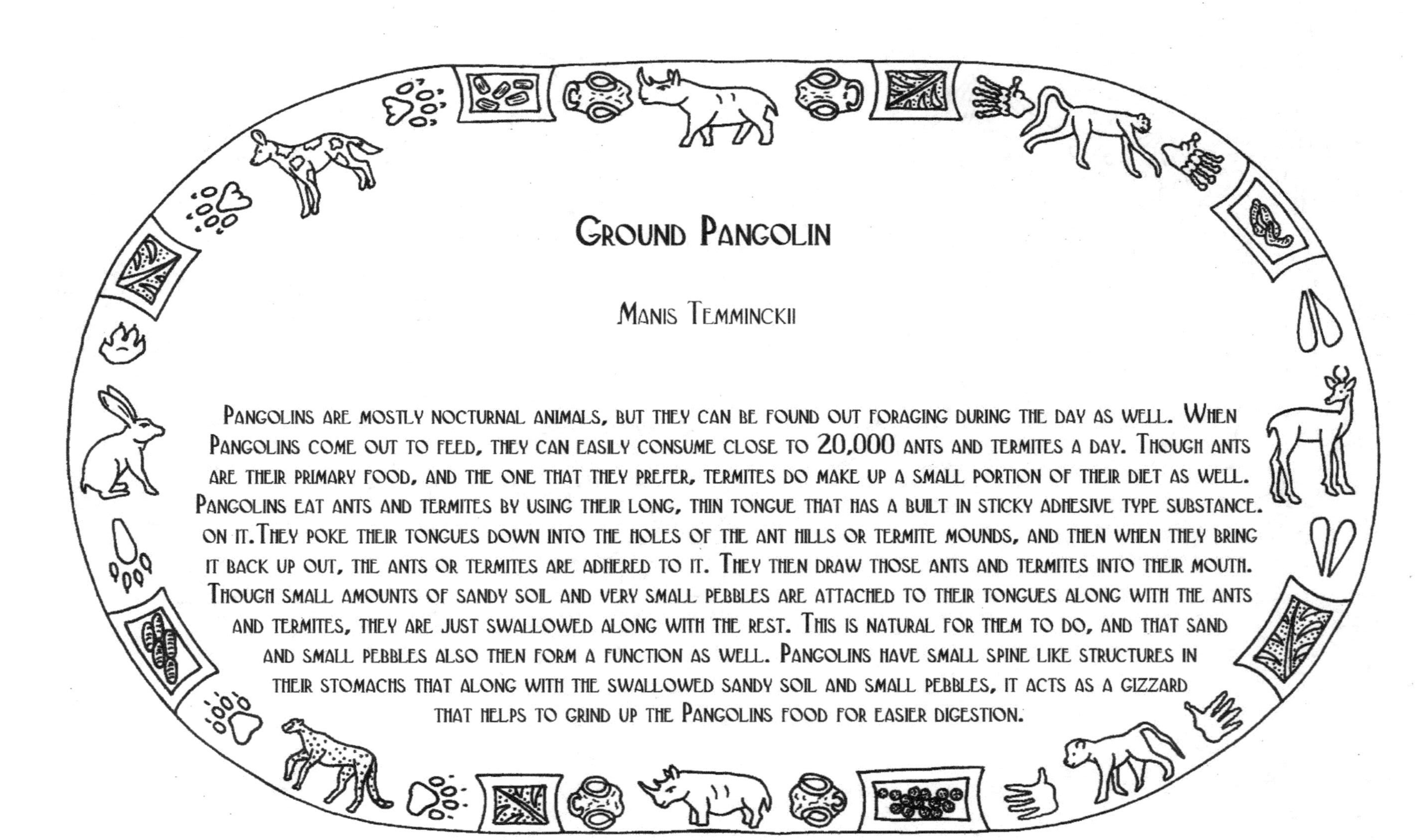

Pangolins are mostly nocturnal animals, but they can be found out foraging during the day as well. When Pangolins come out to feed, they can easily consume close to 20,000 ants and termites a day. Though ants are their primary food, and the one that they prefer, termites do make up a small portion of their diet as well. Pangolins eat ants and termites by using their long, thin tongue that has a built in sticky adhesive type substance. on it. They poke their tongues down into the holes of the ant hills or termite mounds, and then when they bring it back up out, the ants or termites are adhered to it. They then draw those ants and termites into their mouth. Though small amounts of sandy soil and very small pebbles are attached to their tongues along with the ants and termites, they are just swallowed along with the rest. This is natural for them to do, and that sand and small pebbles also then form a function as well. Pangolins have small spine like structures in their stomachs that along with the swallowed sandy soil and small pebbles, it acts as a gizzard that helps to grind up the Pangolins food for easier digestion.

Ground Pangolin

Manis Temminckii

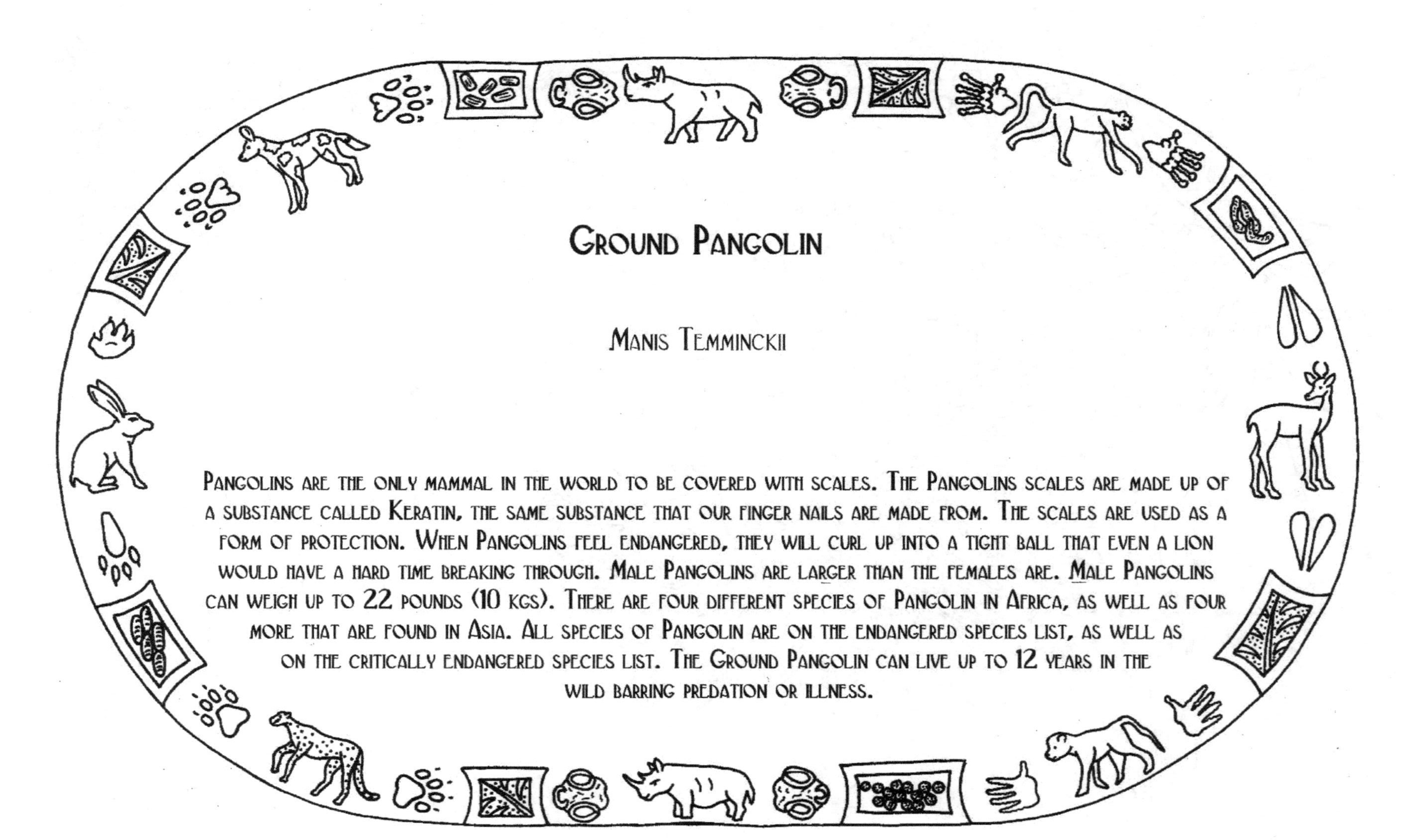

Pangolins are the only mammal in the world to be covered with scales. The Pangolins scales are made up of a substance called Keratin, the same substance that our finger nails are made from. The scales are used as a form of protection. When Pangolins feel endangered, they will curl up into a tight ball that even a lion would have a hard time breaking through. Male Pangolins are larger than the females are. Male Pangolins can weigh up to 22 pounds (10 kgs). There are four different species of Pangolin in Africa, as well as four more that are found in Asia. All species of Pangolin are on the endangered species list, as well as on the critically endangered species list. The Ground Pangolin can live up to 12 years in the wild barring predation or illness.

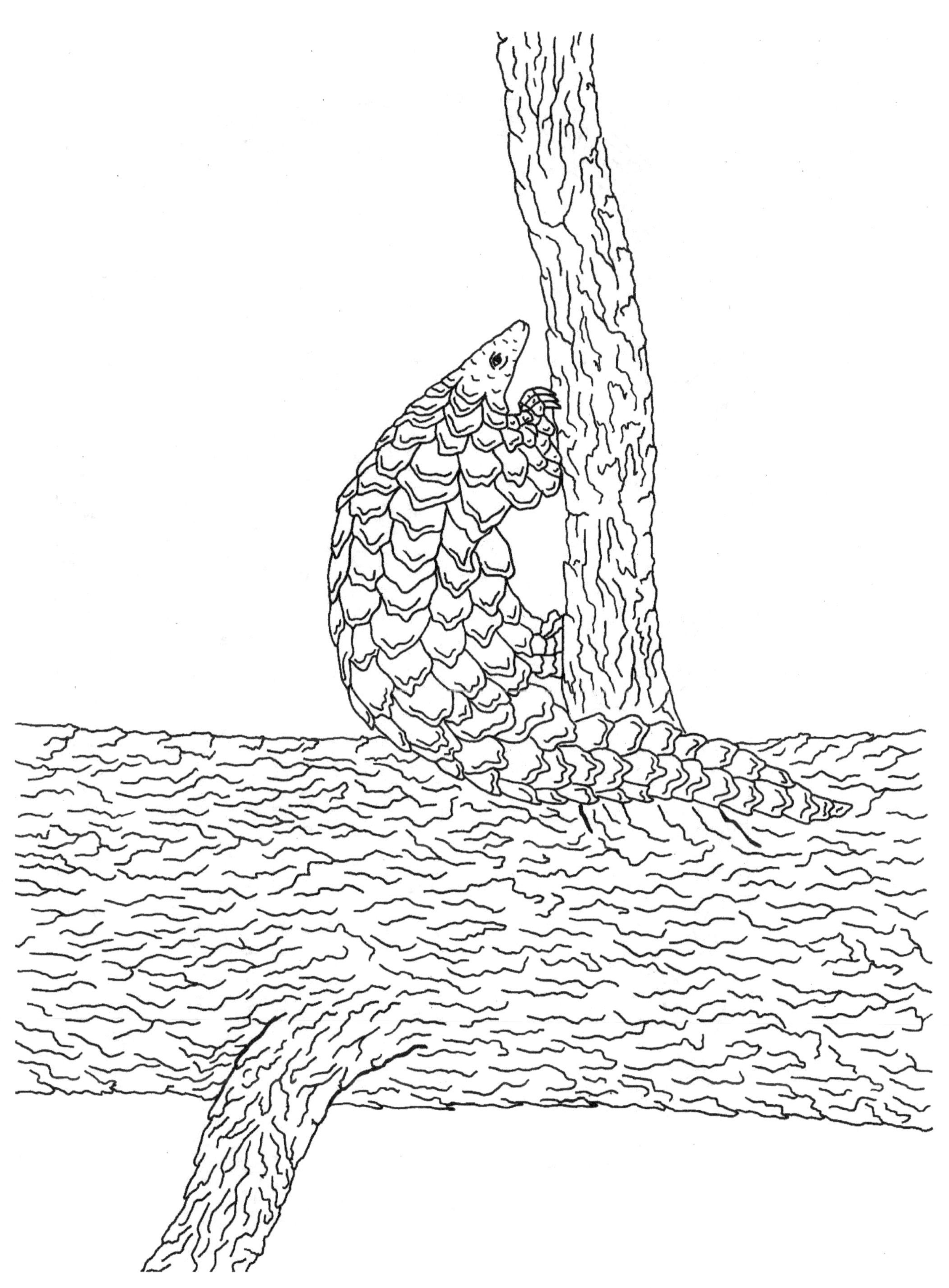

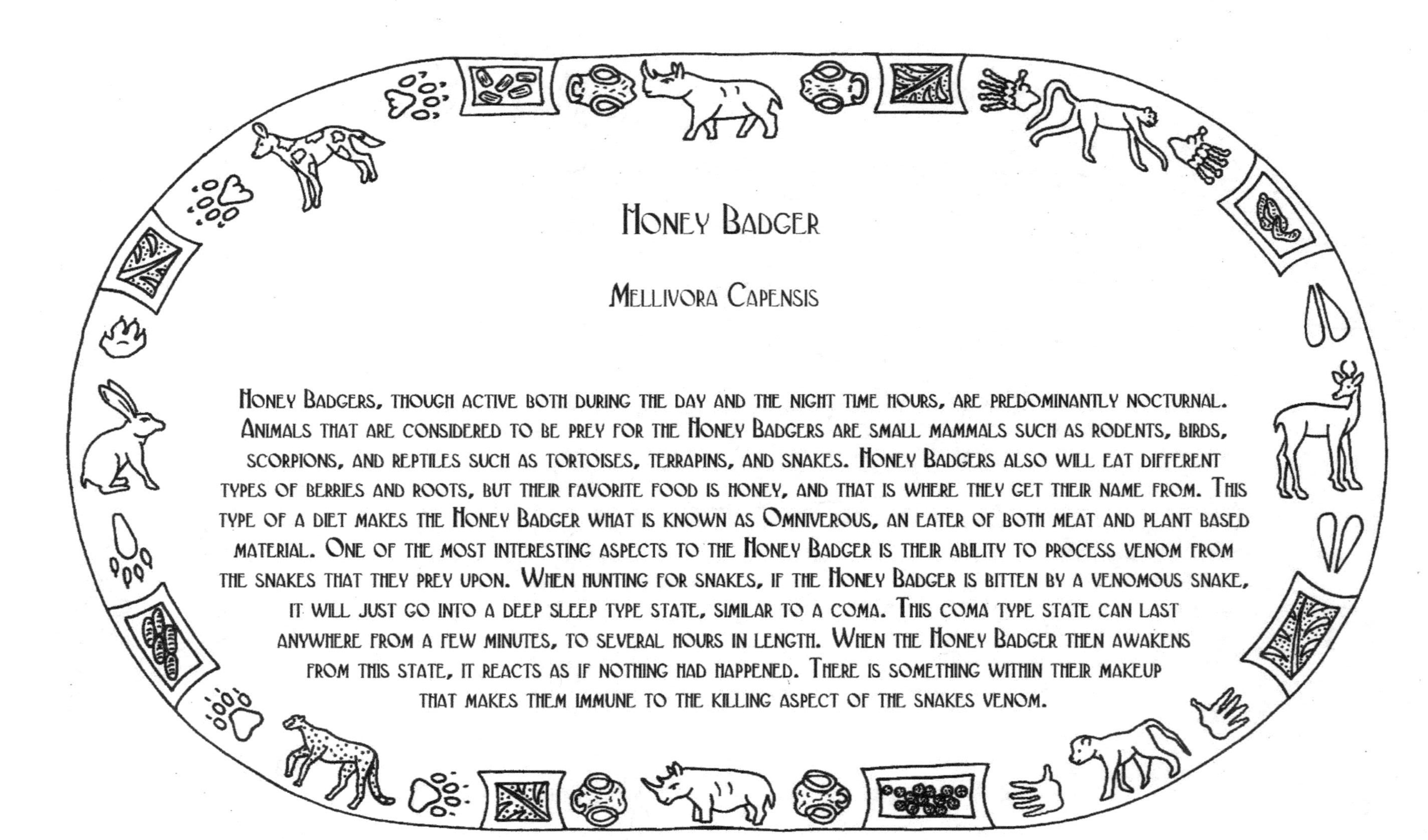

Honey Badger

Mellivora Capensis

Honey Badgers, though active both during the day and the night time hours, are predominantly nocturnal. Animals that are considered to be prey for the Honey Badgers are small mammals such as rodents, birds, scorpions, and reptiles such as tortoises, terrapins, and snakes. Honey Badgers also will eat different types of berries and roots, but their favorite food is honey, and that is where they get their name from. This type of a diet makes the Honey Badger what is known as Omniverous, an eater of both meat and plant based material. One of the most interesting aspects to the Honey Badger is their ability to process venom from the snakes that they prey upon. When hunting for snakes, if the Honey Badger is bitten by a venomous snake, it will just go into a deep sleep type state, similar to a coma. This coma type state can last anywhere from a few minutes, to several hours in length. When the Honey Badger then awakens from this state, it reacts as if nothing had happened. There is something within their makeup that makes them immune to the killing aspect of the snakes venom.

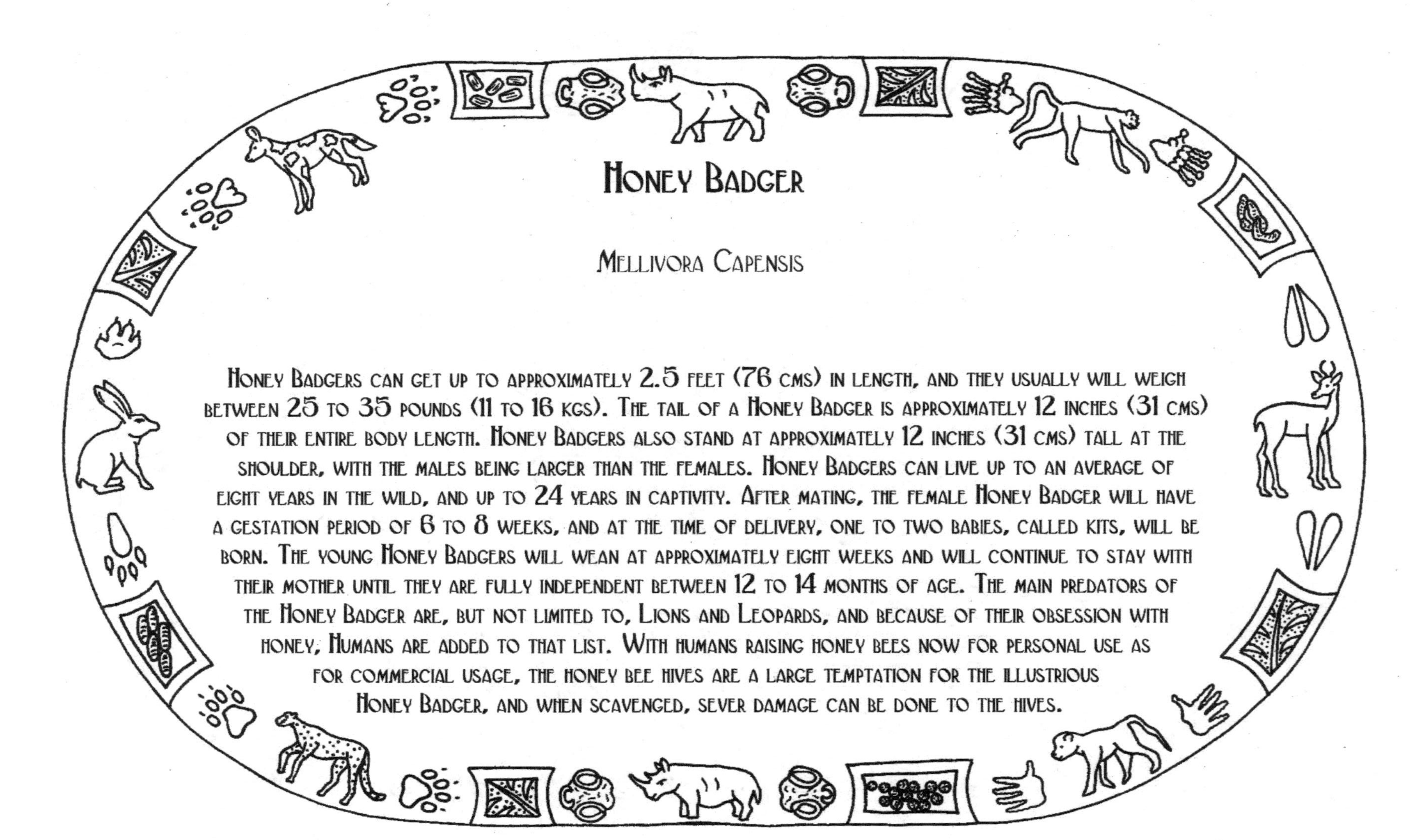

Honey Badger

Mellivora Capensis

Honey Badgers can get up to approximately 2.5 feet (76 cms) in length, and they usually will weigh between 25 to 35 pounds (11 to 16 kgs). The tail of a Honey Badger is approximately 12 inches (31 cms) of their entire body length. Honey Badgers also stand at approximately 12 inches (31 cms) tall at the shoulder, with the males being larger than the females. Honey Badgers can live up to an average of eight years in the wild, and up to 24 years in captivity. After mating, the female Honey Badger will have a gestation period of 6 to 8 weeks, and at the time of delivery, one to two babies, called kits, will be born. The young Honey Badgers will wean at approximately eight weeks and will continue to stay with their mother until they are fully independent between 12 to 14 months of age. The main predators of the Honey Badger are, but not limited to, Lions and Leopards, and because of their obsession with honey, Humans are added to that list. With humans raising honey bees now for personal use as for commercial usage, the honey bee hives are a large temptation for the illustrious Honey Badger, and when scavenged, sever damage can be done to the hives.

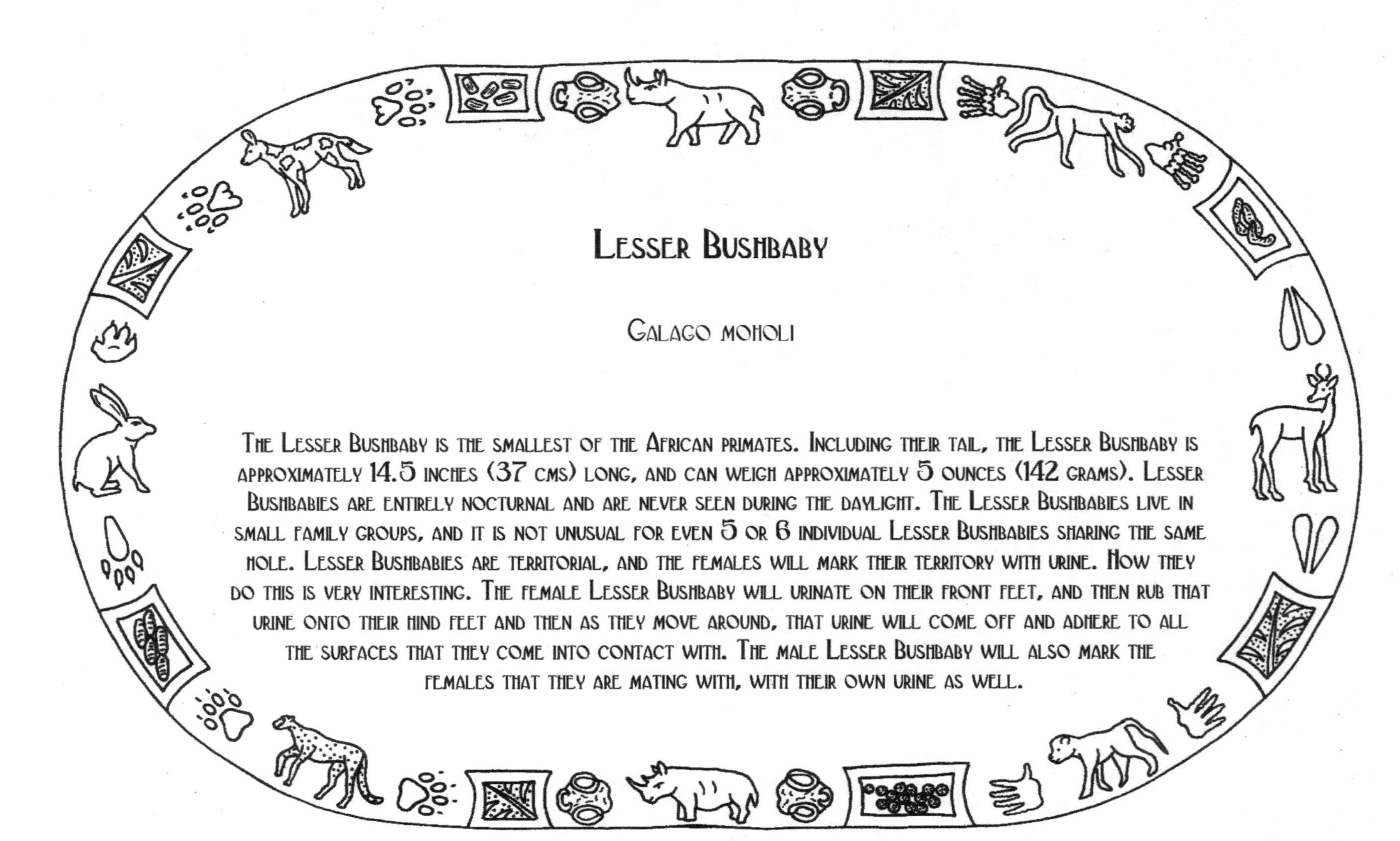

Lesser Bushbaby

Galago moholi

The Lesser Bushbaby is the smallest of the African primates. Including their tail, the Lesser Bushbaby is approximately 14.5 inches (37 cms) long, and can weigh approximately 5 ounces (142 grams). Lesser Bushbabies are entirely nocturnal and are never seen during the daylight. The Lesser Bushbabies live in small family groups, and it is not unusual for even 5 or 6 individual Lesser Bushbabies sharing the same hole. Lesser Bushbabies are territorial, and the females will mark their territory with urine. How they do this is very interesting. The female Lesser Bushbaby will urinate on their front feet, and then rub that urine onto their hind feet and then as they move around, that urine will come off and adhere to all the surfaces that they come into contact with. The male Lesser Bushbaby will also mark the females that they are mating with, with their own urine as well.

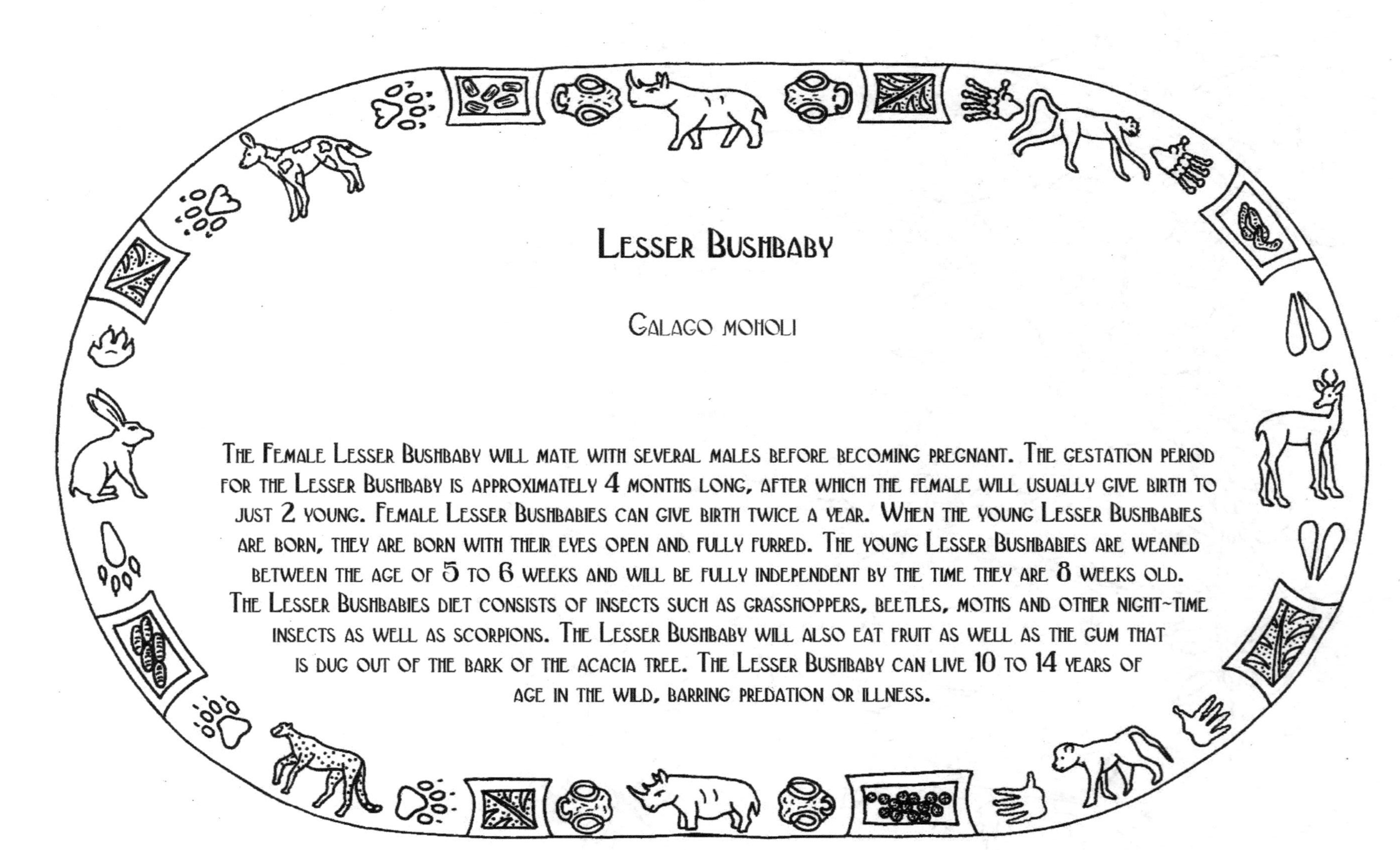

Lesser Bushbaby

Galago moholi

The Female Lesser Bushbaby will mate with several males before becoming pregnant. The gestation period for the Lesser Bushbaby is approximately 4 months long, after which the female will usually give birth to just 2 young. Female Lesser Bushbabies can give birth twice a year. When the young Lesser Bushbabies are born, they are born with their eyes open and fully furred. The young Lesser Bushbabies are weaned between the age of 5 to 6 weeks and will be fully independent by the time they are 8 weeks old. The Lesser Bushbabies diet consists of insects such as grasshoppers, beetles, moths and other night~time insects as well as scorpions. The Lesser Bushbaby will also eat fruit as well as the gum that is dug out of the bark of the acacia tree. The Lesser Bushbaby can live 10 to 14 years of age in the wild, barring predation or illness.

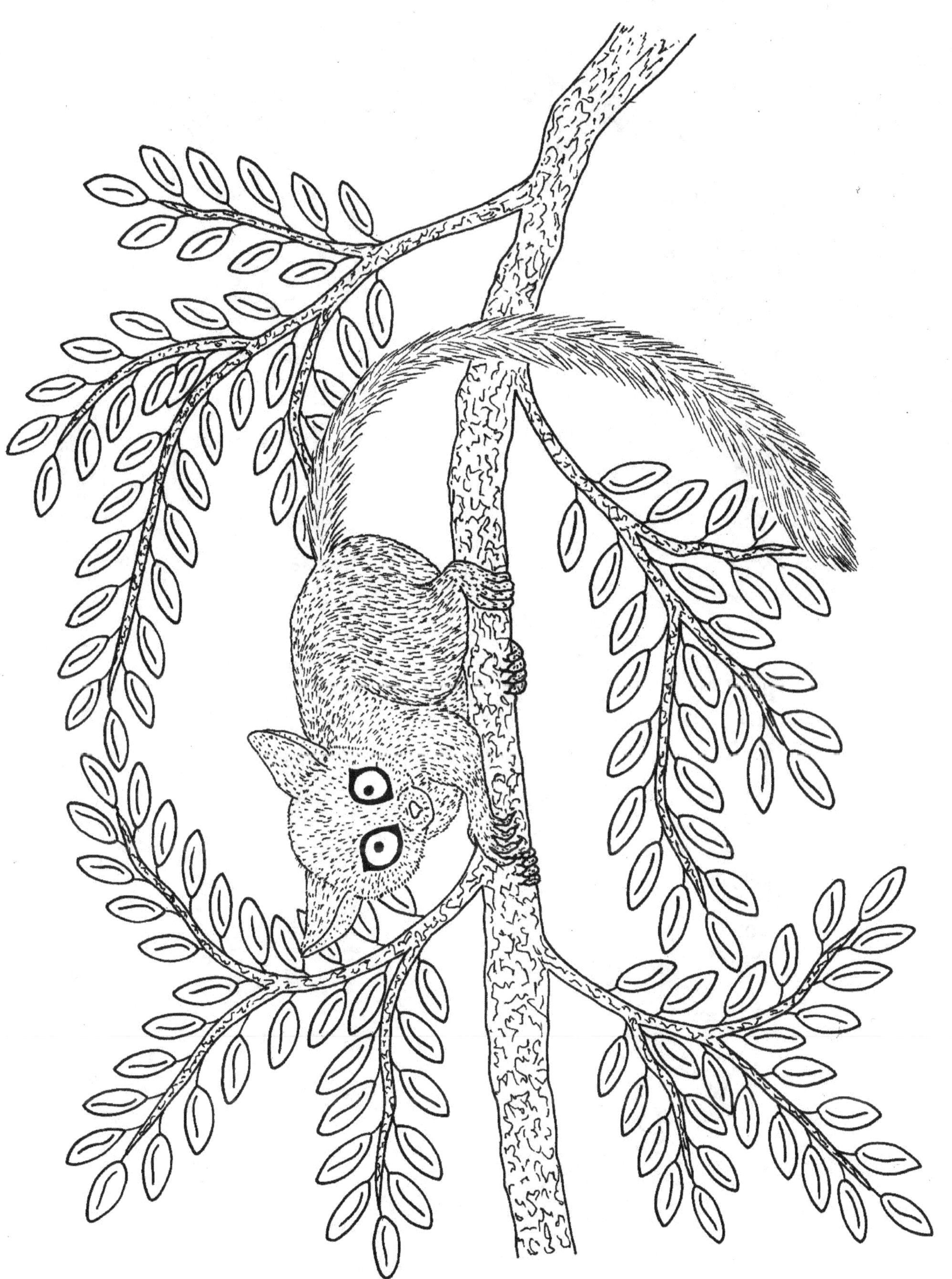

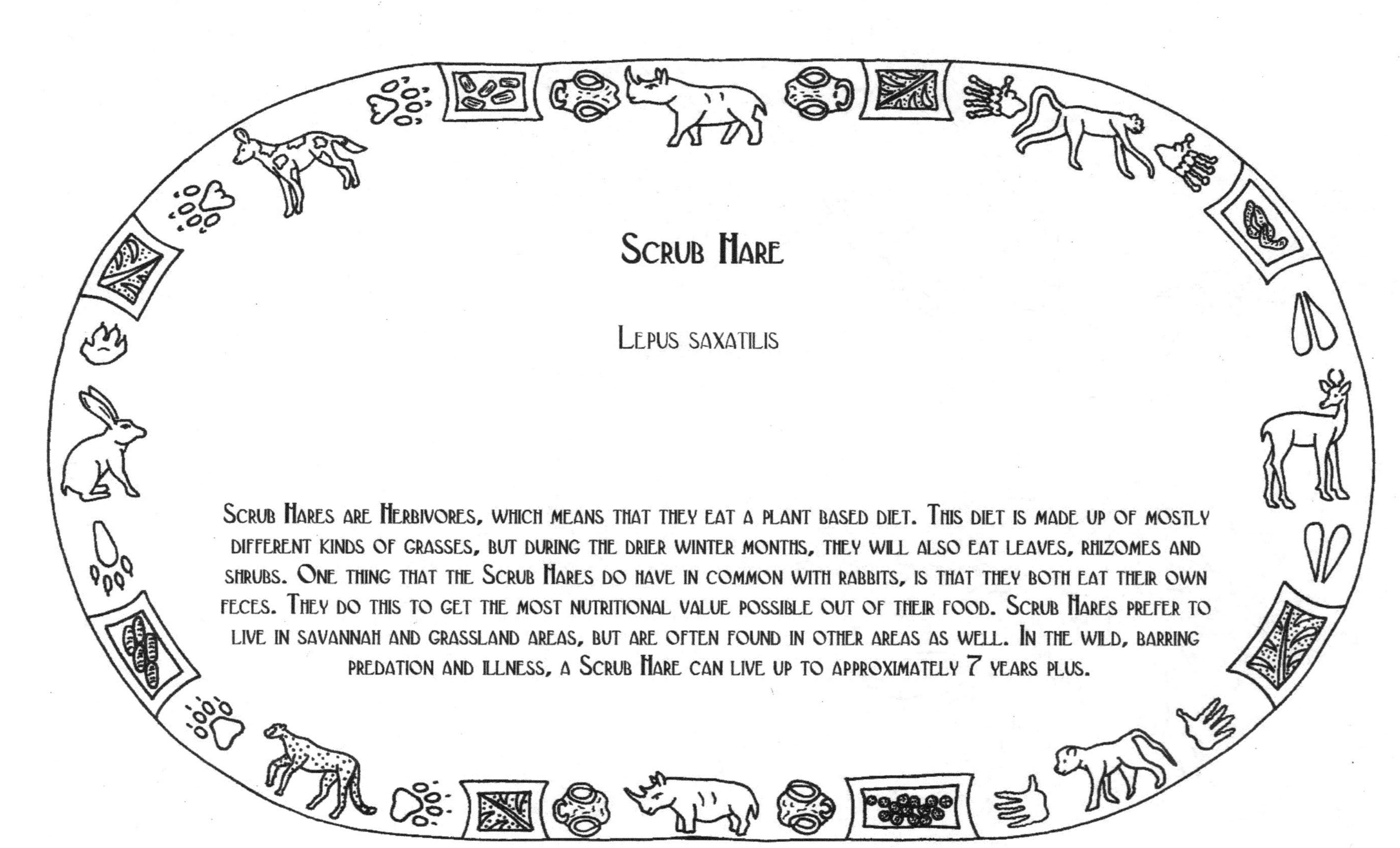

Scrub Hare

Lepus saxatilis

Scrub Hares are Herbivores, which means that they eat a plant based diet. This diet is made up of mostly different kinds of grasses, but during the drier winter months, they will also eat leaves, rhizomes and shrubs. One thing that the Scrub Hares do have in common with rabbits, is that they both eat their own feces. They do this to get the most nutritional value possible out of their food. Scrub Hares prefer to live in savannah and grassland areas, but are often found in other areas as well. In the wild, barring predation and illness, a Scrub Hare can live up to approximately 7 years plus.

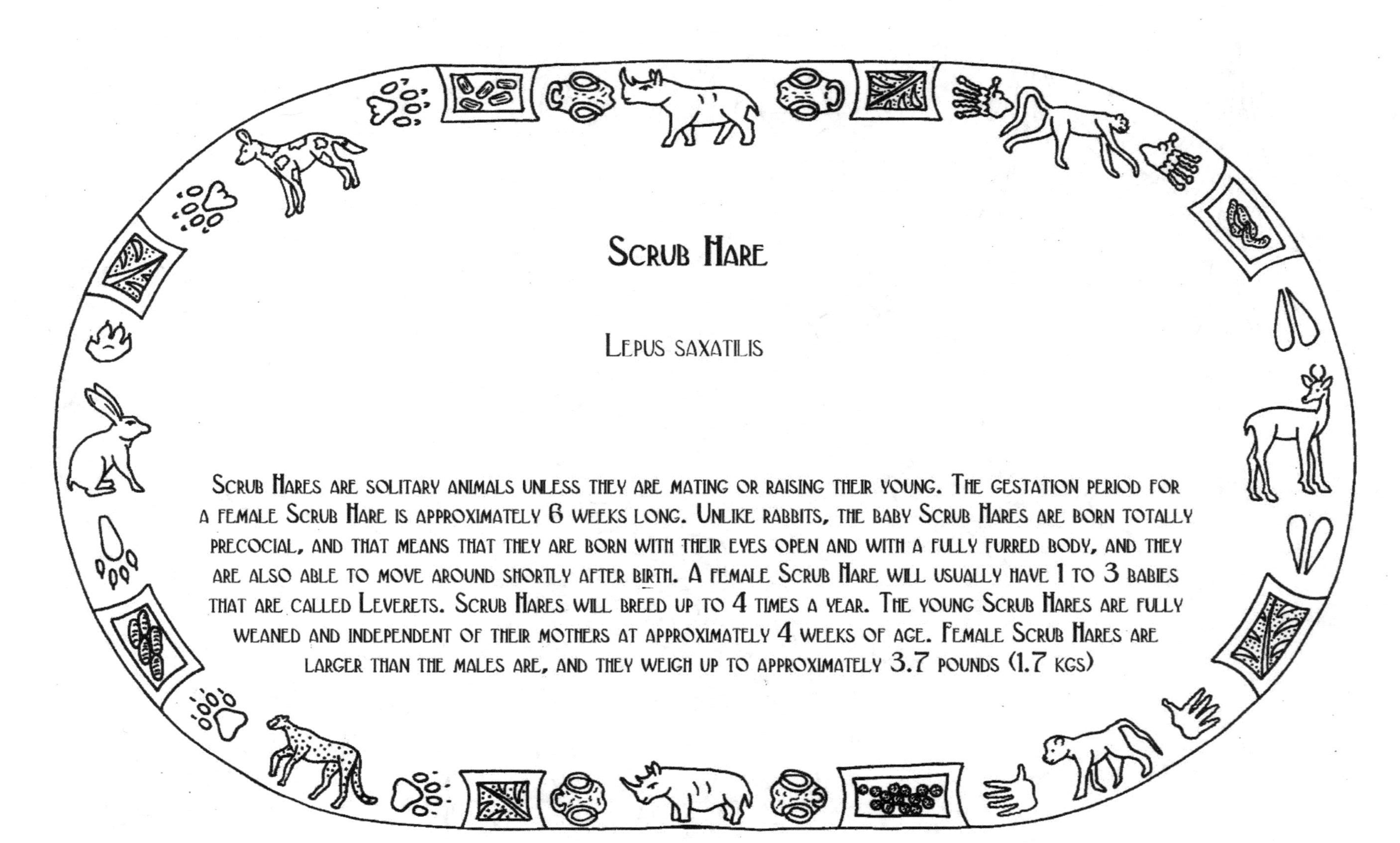

Scrub Hare

Lepus saxatilis

Scrub Hares are solitary animals unless they are mating or raising their young. The gestation period for a female Scrub Hare is approximately 6 weeks long. Unlike rabbits, the baby Scrub Hares are born totally precocial, and that means that they are born with their eyes open and with a fully furred body, and they are also able to move around shortly after birth. A female Scrub Hare will usually have 1 to 3 babies that are called Leverets. Scrub Hares will breed up to 4 times a year. The young Scrub Hares are fully weaned and independent of their mothers at approximately 4 weeks of age. Female Scrub Hares are larger than the males are, and they weigh up to approximately 3.7 pounds (1.7 kgs)

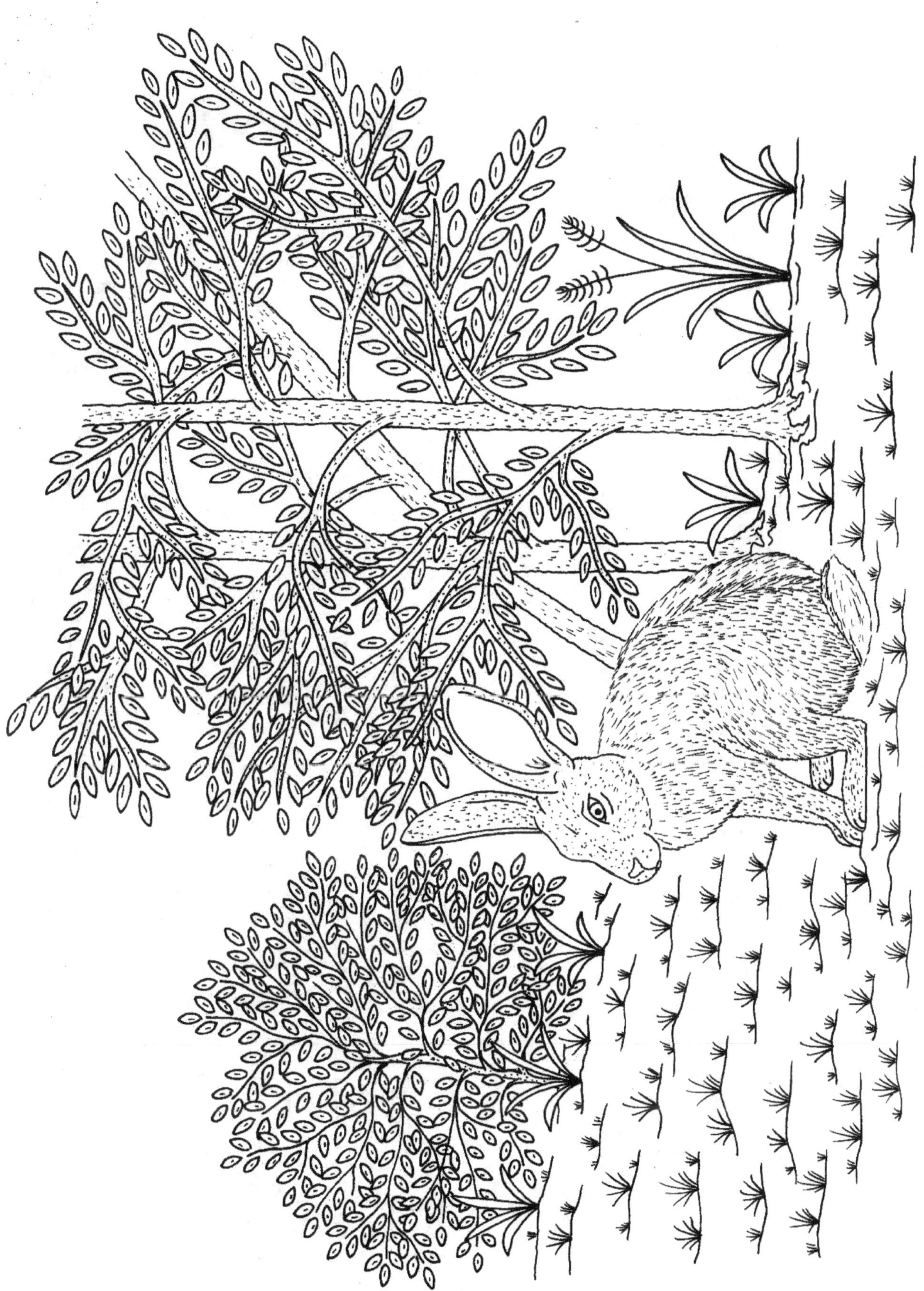

Serval

Felis Serval

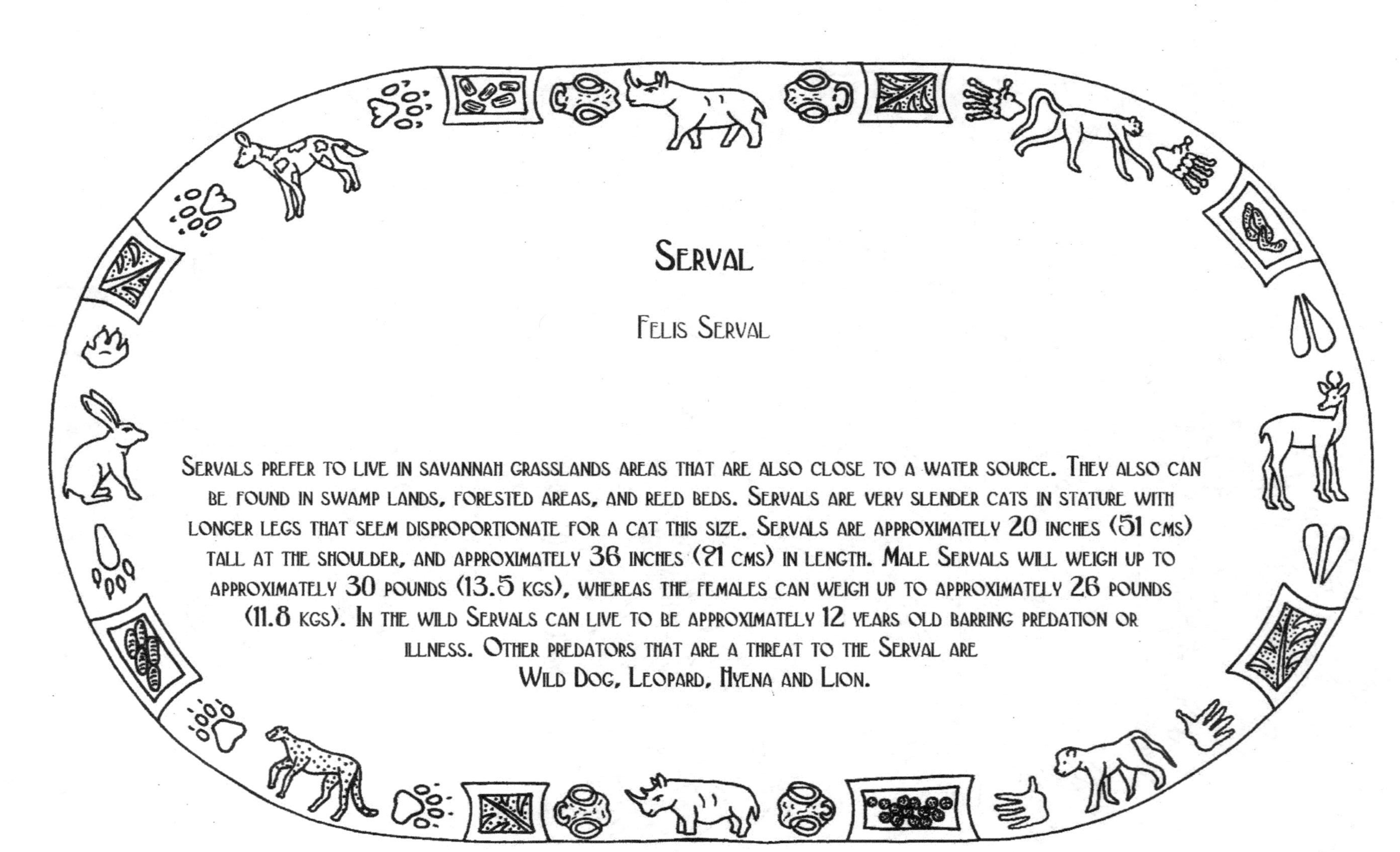

Servals prefer to live in savannah grasslands areas that are also close to a water source. They also can be found in swamp lands, forested areas, and reed beds. Servals are very slender cats in stature with longer legs that seem disproportionate for a cat this size. Servals are approximately 20 inches (51 cms) tall at the shoulder, and approximately 36 inches (91 cms) in length. Male Servals will weigh up to approximately 30 pounds (13.5 kgs), whereas the females can weigh up to approximately 26 pounds (11.8 kgs). In the wild Servals can live to be approximately 12 years old barring predation or illness. Other predators that are a threat to the Serval are Wild Dog, Leopard, Hyena and Lion.

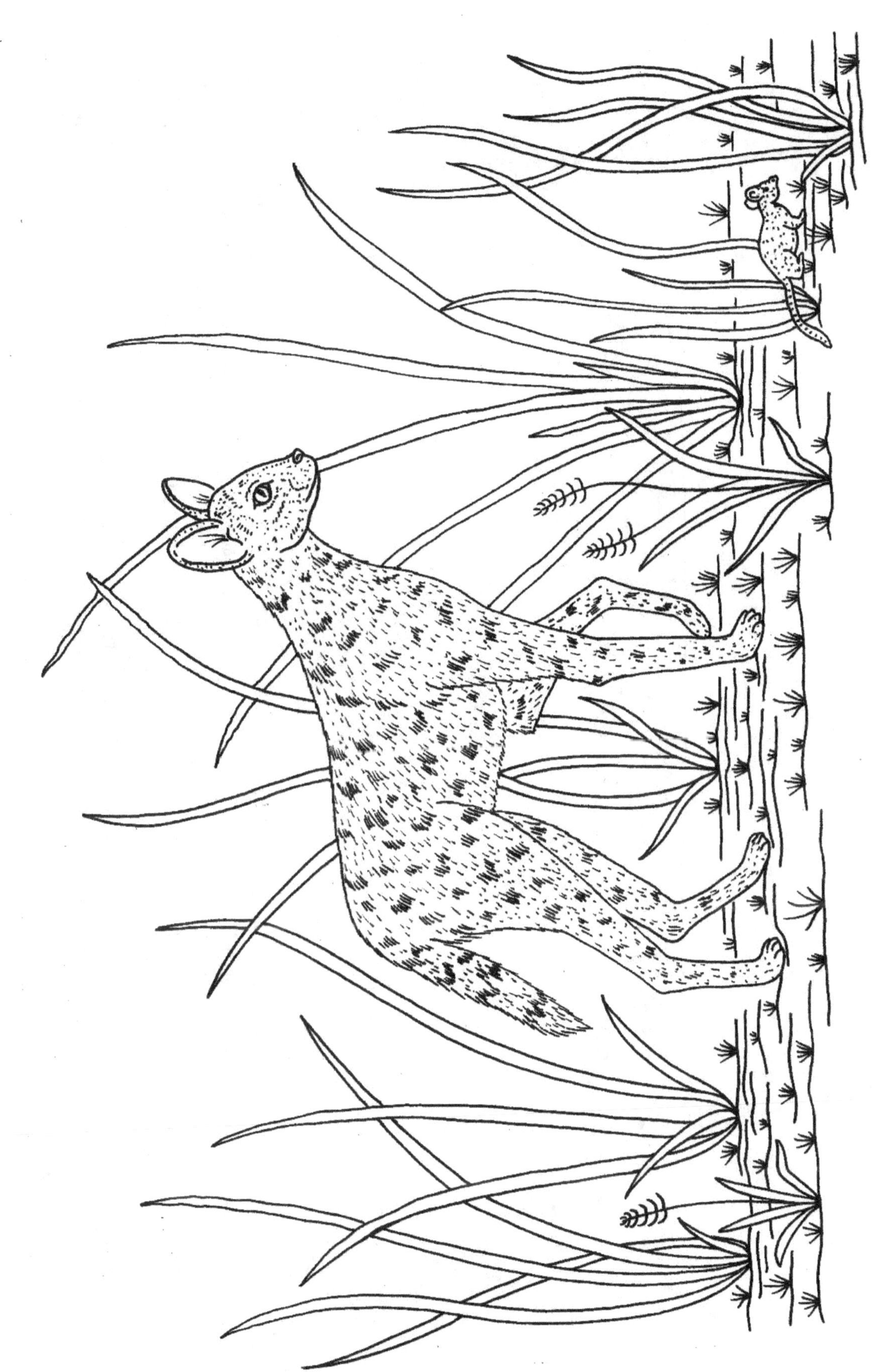

Serval

Felis Serval

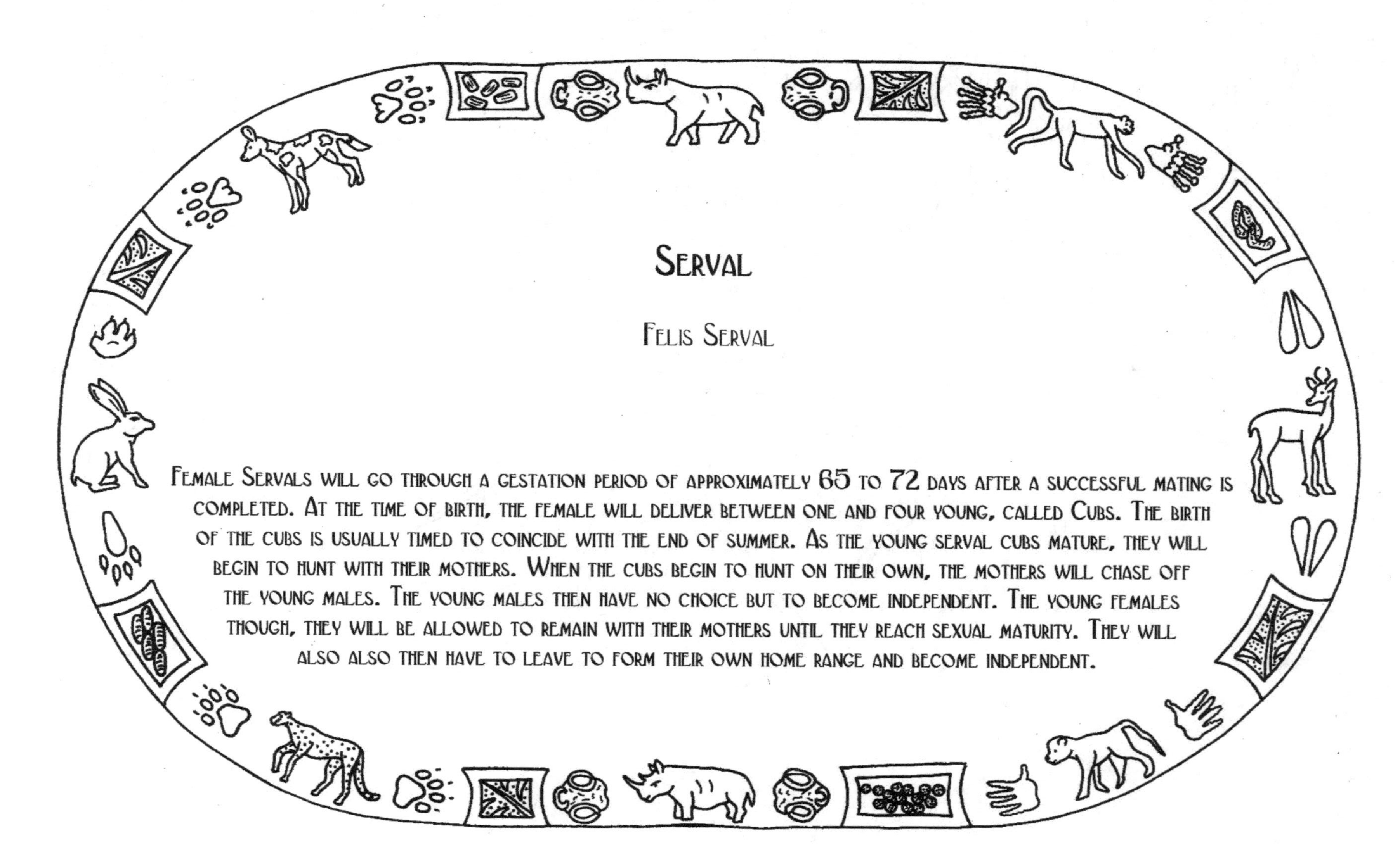

Female Servals will go through a gestation period of approximately 65 to 72 days after a successful mating is completed. At the time of birth, the female will deliver between one and four young, called Cubs. The birth of the cubs is usually timed to coincide with the end of summer. As the young serval cubs mature, they will begin to hunt with their mothers. When the cubs begin to hunt on their own, the mothers will chase off the young males. The young males then have no choice but to become independent. The young females though, they will be allowed to remain with their mothers until they reach sexual maturity. They will also also then have to leave to form their own home range and become independent.

Serval

Felis Serval

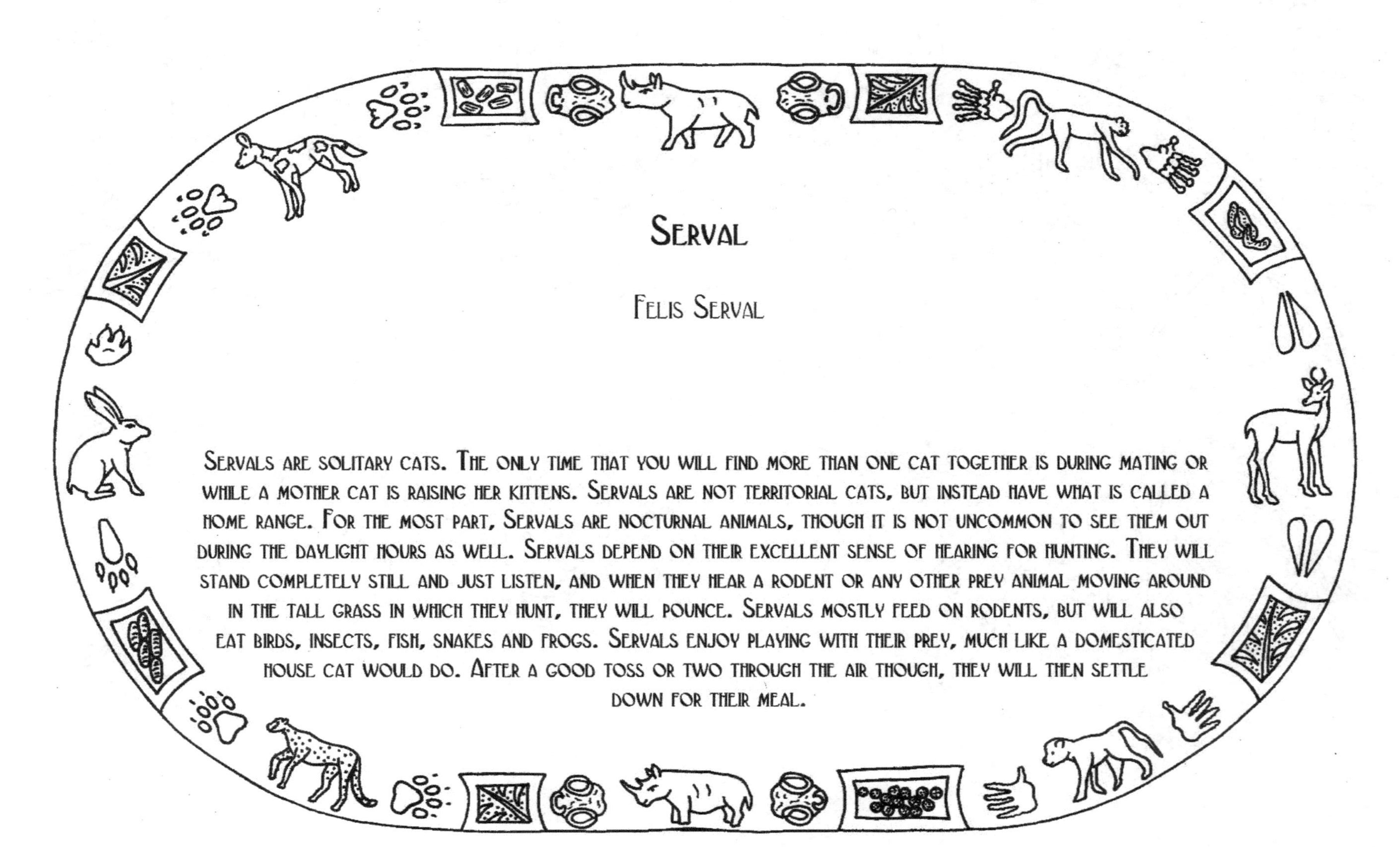

Servals are solitary cats. The only time that you will find more than one cat together is during mating or while a mother cat is raising her kittens. Servals are not territorial cats, but instead have what is called a home range. For the most part, Servals are nocturnal animals, though it is not uncommon to see them out during the daylight hours as well. Servals depend on their excellent sense of hearing for hunting. They will stand completely still and just listen, and when they hear a rodent or any other prey animal moving around in the tall grass in which they hunt, they will pounce. Servals mostly feed on rodents, but will also eat birds, insects, fish, snakes and frogs. Servals enjoy playing with their prey, much like a domesticated house cat would do. After a good toss or two through the air though, they will then settle down for their meal.

Side~Striped Jackal

Canisadjustus

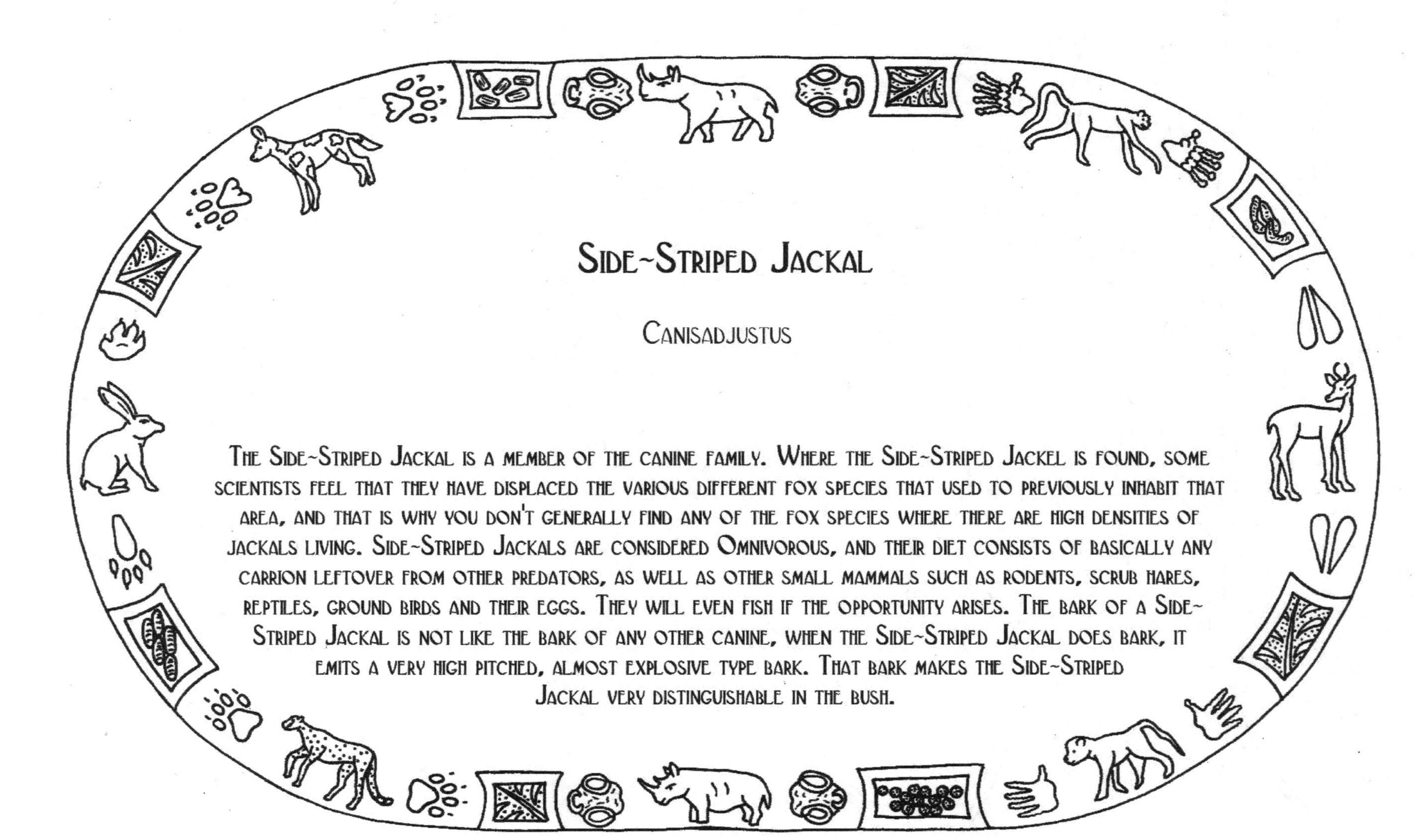

The Side~Striped Jackal is a member of the canine family. Where the Side~Striped Jackel is found, some scientists feel that they have displaced the various different fox species that used to previously inhabit that area, and that is why you don't generally find any of the fox species where there are high densities of jackals living. Side~Striped Jackals are considered Omnivorous, and their diet consists of basically any carrion leftover from other predators, as well as other small mammals such as rodents, scrub hares, reptiles, ground birds and their eggs. They will even fish if the opportunity arises. The bark of a Side~Striped Jackal is not like the bark of any other canine, when the Side~Striped Jackal does bark, it emits a very high pitched, almost explosive type bark. That bark makes the Side~Striped Jackal very distinguishable in the bush.

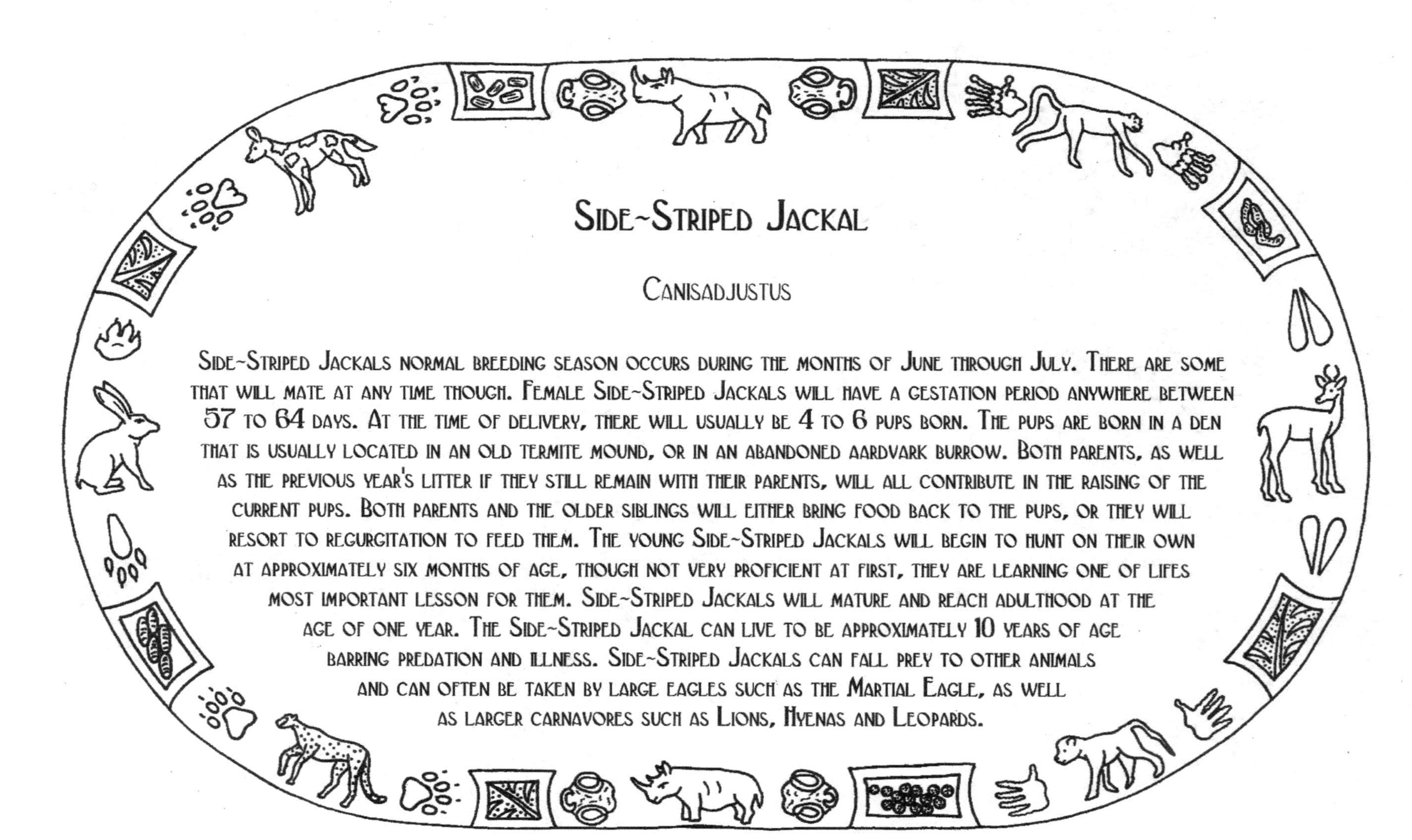

Side~Striped Jackal

Canisadjustus

Side~Striped Jackals normal breeding season occurs during the months of June through July. There are some that will mate at any time though. Female Side~Striped Jackals will have a gestation period anywhere between 57 to 64 days. At the time of delivery, there will usually be 4 to 6 pups born. The pups are born in a den that is usually located in an old termite mound, or in an abandoned aardvark burrow. Both parents, as well as the previous year's litter if they still remain with their parents, will all contribute in the raising of the current pups. Both parents and the older siblings will either bring food back to the pups, or they will resort to regurgitation to feed them. The young Side~Striped Jackals will begin to hunt on their own at approximately six months of age, though not very proficient at first, they are learning one of lifes most important lesson for them. Side~Striped Jackals will mature and reach adulthood at the age of one year. The Side~Striped Jackal can live to be approximately 10 years of age barring predation and illness. Side~Striped Jackals can fall prey to other animals and can often be taken by large eagles such as the Martial Eagle, as well as larger carnavores such as Lions, Hyenas and Leopards.

Side~Striped Jackal

Canisadjustus

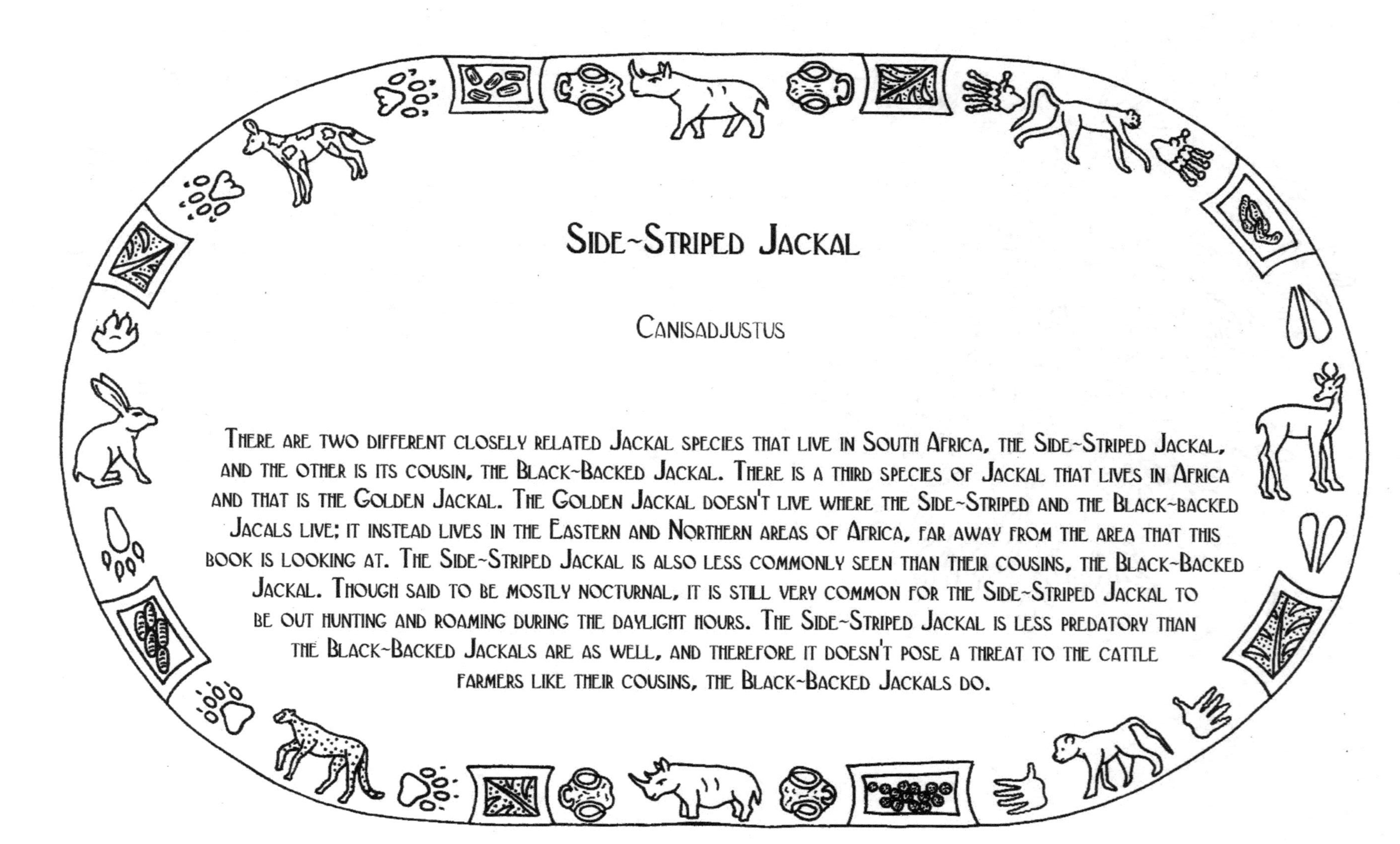

There are two different closely related Jackal species that live in South Africa, the Side~Striped Jackal, and the other is its cousin, the Black~Backed Jackal. There is a third species of Jackal that lives in Africa and that is the Golden Jackal. The Golden Jackal doesn't live where the Side~Striped and the Black~backed Jacals live; it instead lives in the Eastern and Northern areas of Africa, far away from the area that this book is looking at. The Side~Striped Jackal is also less commonly seen than their cousins, the Black~Backed Jackal. Though said to be mostly nocturnal, it is still very common for the Side~Striped Jackal to be out hunting and roaming during the daylight hours. The Side~Striped Jackal is less predatory than the Black~Backed Jackals are as well, and therefore it doesn't pose a threat to the cattle farmers like their cousins, the Black~Backed Jackals do.

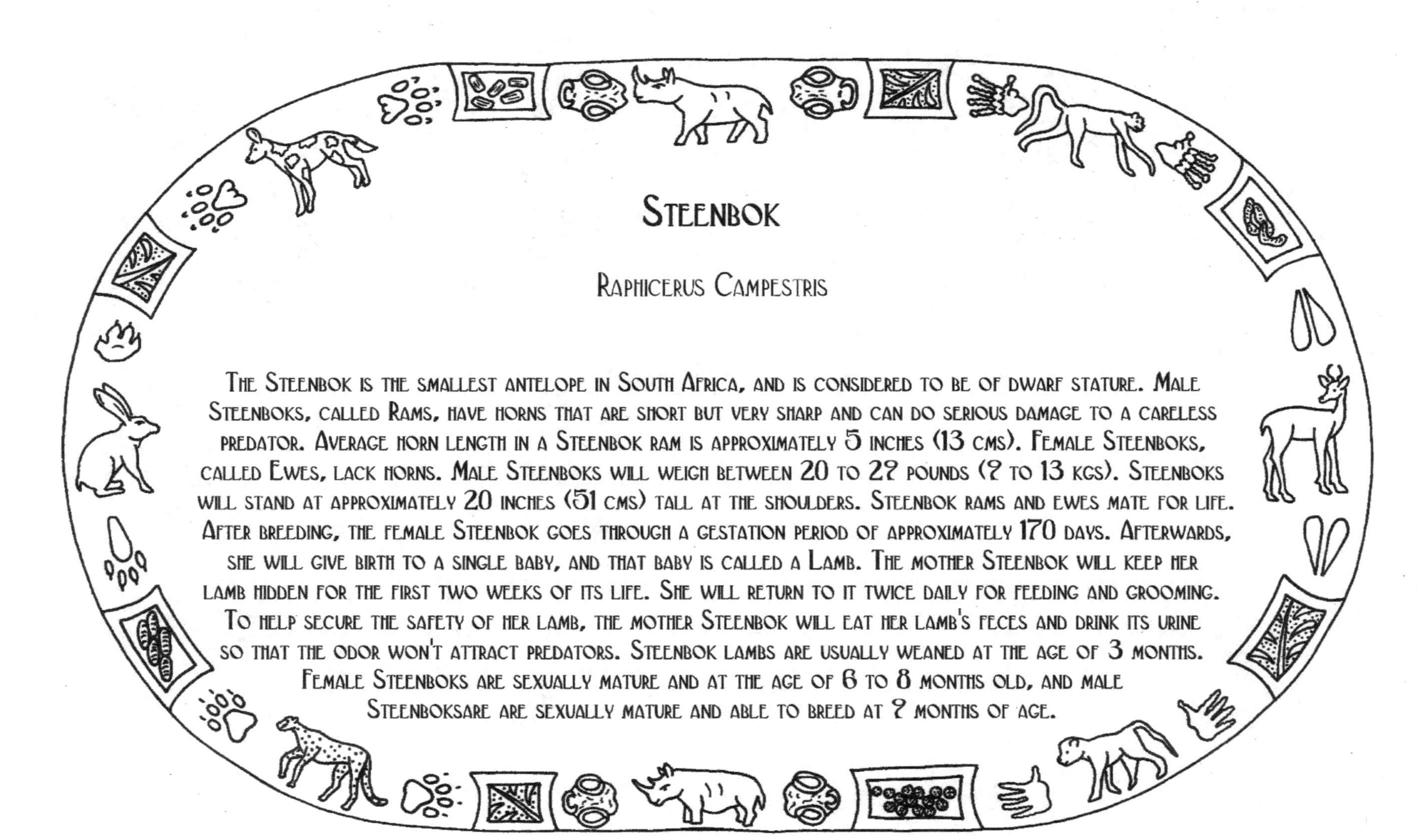

Steenbok

Raphicerus Campestris

The Steenbok is the smallest antelope in South Africa, and is considered to be of dwarf stature. Male Steenboks, called Rams, have horns that are short but very sharp and can do serious damage to a careless predator. Average horn length in a Steenbok ram is approximately 5 inches (13 cms). Female Steenboks, called Ewes, lack horns. Male Steenboks will weigh between 20 to 28 pounds (9 to 13 kgs). Steenboks will stand at approximately 20 inches (51 cms) tall at the shoulders. Steenbok rams and ewes mate for life. After breeding, the female Steenbok goes through a gestation period of approximately 170 days. Afterwards, she will give birth to a single baby, and that baby is called a Lamb. The mother Steenbok will keep her lamb hidden for the first two weeks of its life. She will return to it twice daily for feeding and grooming. To help secure the safety of her lamb, the mother Steenbok will eat her lamb's feces and drink its urine so that the odor won't attract predators. Steenbok lambs are usually weaned at the age of 3 months. Female Steenboks are sexually mature and at the age of 6 to 8 months old, and male Steenboksare are sexually mature and able to breed at 9 months of age.

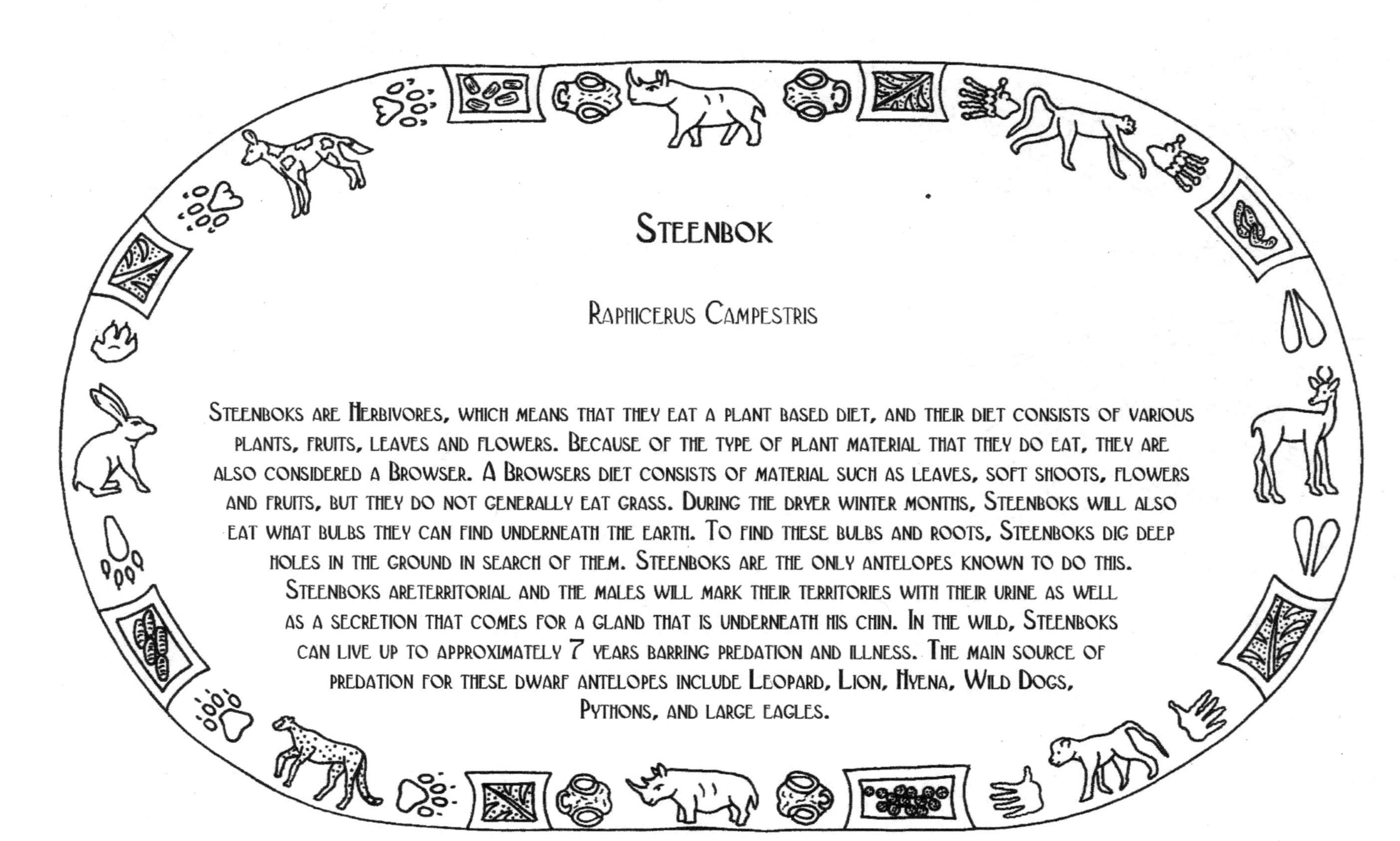

Steenbok

Raphicerus Campestris

Steenboks are Herbivores, which means that they eat a plant based diet, and their diet consists of various plants, fruits, leaves and flowers. Because of the type of plant material that they do eat, they are also considered a Browser. A Browsers diet consists of material such as leaves, soft shoots, flowers and fruits, but they do not generally eat grass. During the dryer winter months, Steenboks will also eat what bulbs they can find underneath the earth. To find these bulbs and roots, Steenboks dig deep holes in the ground in search of them. Steenboks are the only antelopes known to do this. Steenboks are territorial and the males will mark their territories with their urine as well as a secretion that comes for a gland that is underneath his chin. In the wild, Steenboks can live up to approximately 7 years barring predation and illness. The main source of predation for these dwarf antelopes include Leopard, Lion, Hyena, Wild Dogs, Pythons, and large eagles.

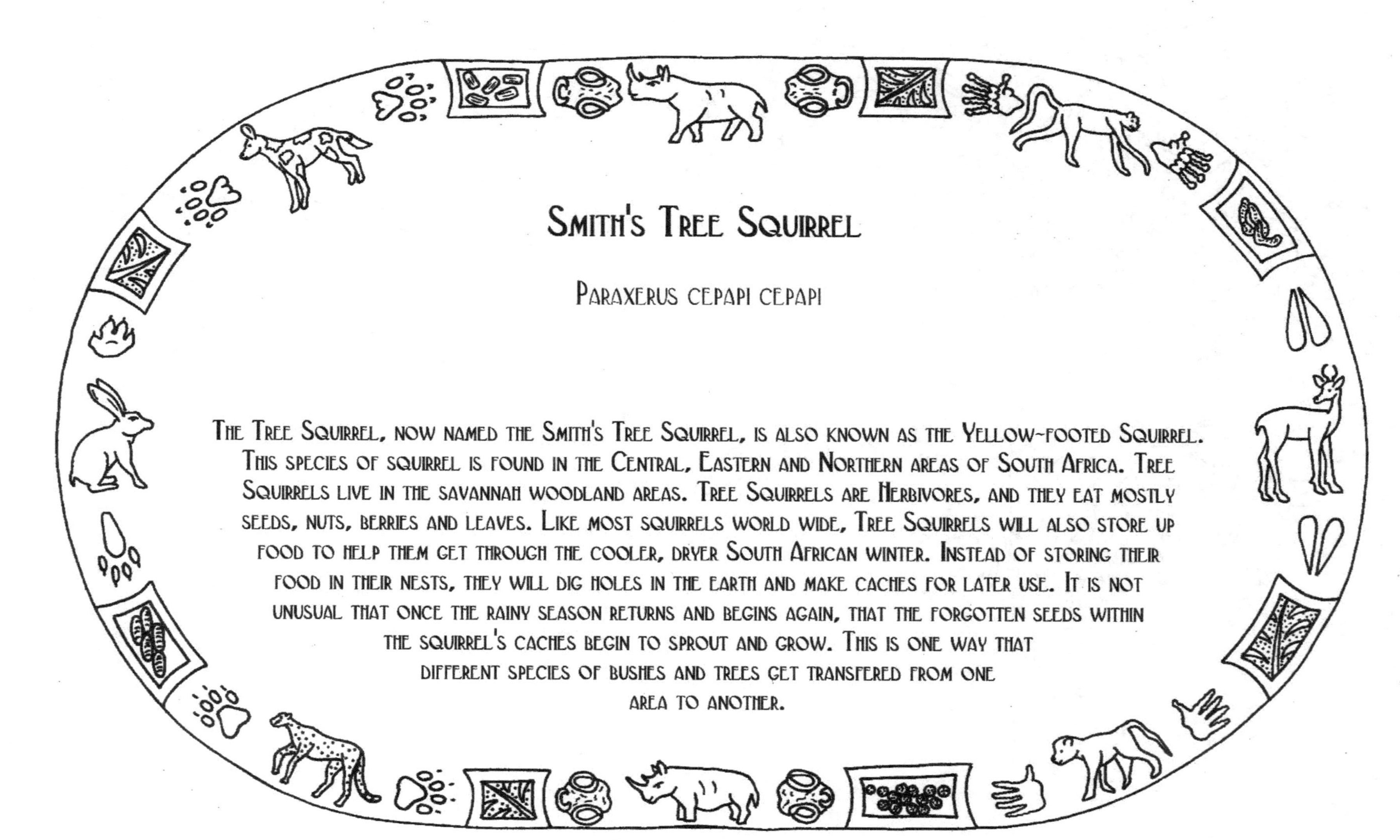

Smith's Tree Squirrel

Paraxerus cepapi cepapi

The Tree Squirrel, now named the Smith's Tree Squirrel, is also known as the Yellow-footed Squirrel. This species of squirrel is found in the Central, Eastern and Northern areas of South Africa. Tree Squirrels live in the savannah woodland areas. Tree Squirrels are Herbivores, and they eat mostly seeds, nuts, berries and leaves. Like most squirrels world wide, Tree Squirrels will also store up food to help them get through the cooler, dryer South African winter. Instead of storing their food in their nests, they will dig holes in the earth and make caches for later use. It is not unusual that once the rainy season returns and begins again, that the forgotten seeds within the squirrel's caches begin to sprout and grow. This is one way that different species of bushes and trees get transfered from one area to another.

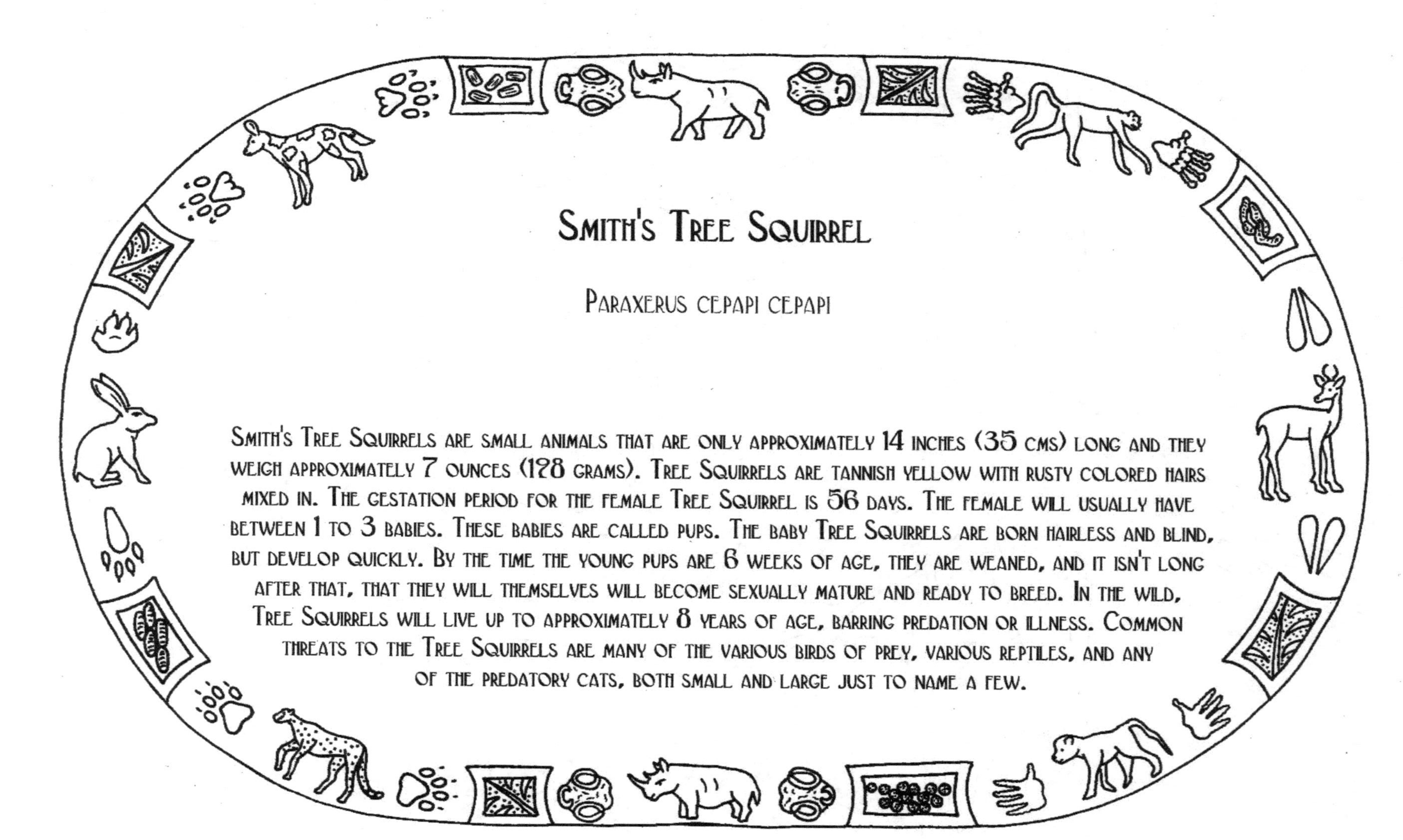

Smith's Tree Squirrel

Paraxerus cepapi cepapi

Smith's Tree Squirrels are small animals that are only approximately 14 inches (35 cms) long and they weigh approximately 7 ounces (128 grams). Tree Squirrels are tannish yellow with rusty colored hairs mixed in. The gestation period for the female Tree Squirrel is 56 days. The female will usually have between 1 to 3 babies. These babies are called pups. The baby Tree Squirrels are born hairless and blind, but develop quickly. By the time the young pups are 6 weeks of age, they are weaned, and it isn't long after that, that they will themselves will become sexually mature and ready to breed. In the wild, Tree Squirrels will live up to approximately 8 years of age, barring predation or illness. Common threats to the Tree Squirrels are many of the various birds of prey, various reptiles, and any of the predatory cats, both small and large just to name a few.

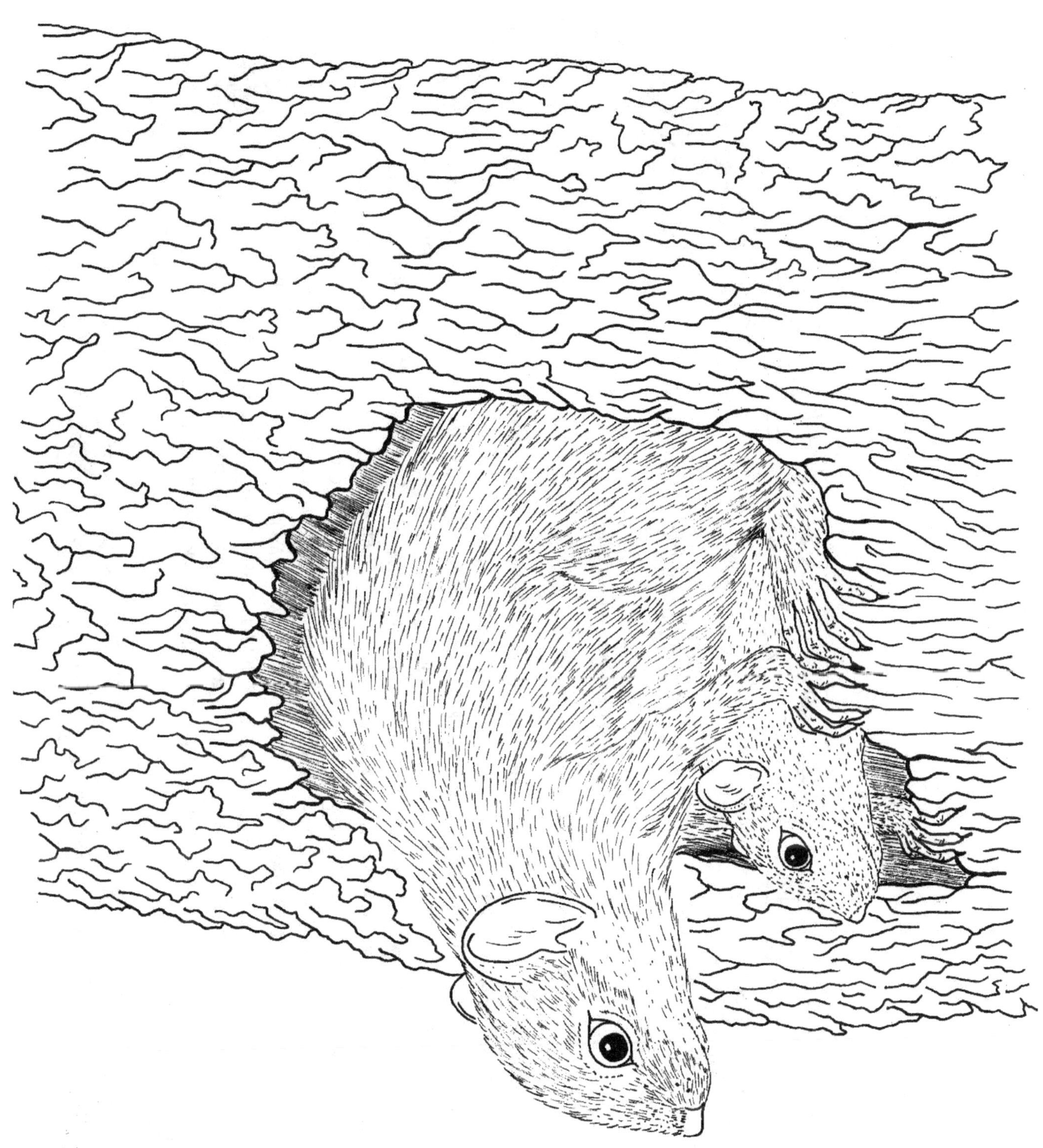

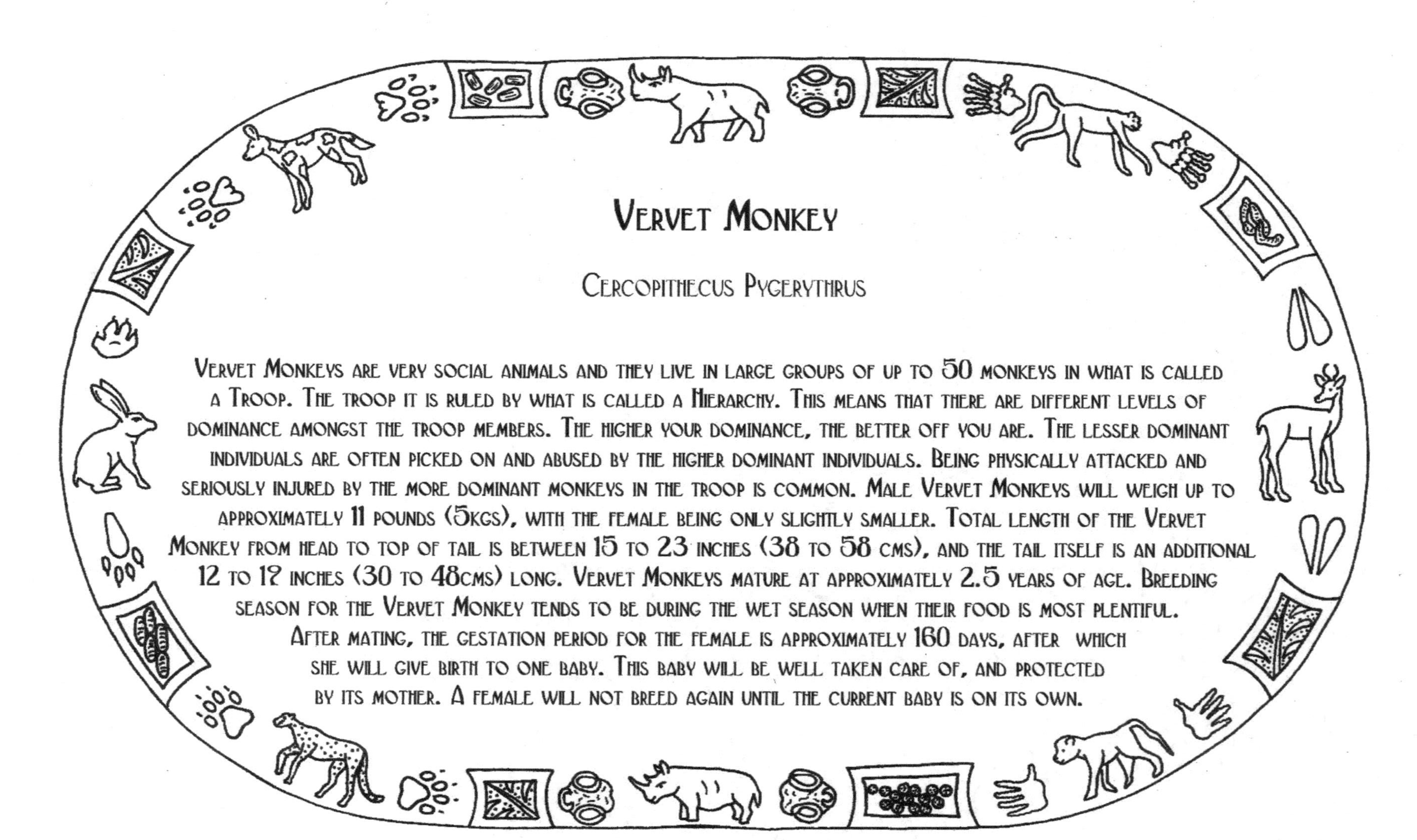

Vervet Monkey

Cercopithecus Pygerythrus

Vervet Monkeys are very social animals and they live in large groups of up to 50 monkeys in what is called a Troop. The troop it is ruled by what is called a Hierarchy. This means that there are different levels of dominance amongst the troop members. The higher your dominance, the better off you are. The lesser dominant individuals are often picked on and abused by the higher dominant individuals. Being physically attacked and seriously injured by the more dominant monkeys in the troop is common. Male Vervet Monkeys will weigh up to approximately 11 pounds (5kgs), with the female being only slightly smaller. Total length of the Vervet Monkey from head to top of tail is between 15 to 23 inches (38 to 58 cms), and the tail itself is an additional 12 to 18 inches (30 to 48cms) long. Vervet Monkeys mature at approximately 2.5 years of age. Breeding season for the Vervet Monkey tends to be during the wet season when their food is most plentiful. After mating, the gestation period for the female is approximately 160 days, after which she will give birth to one baby. This baby will be well taken care of, and protected by its mother. A female will not breed again until the current baby is on its own.

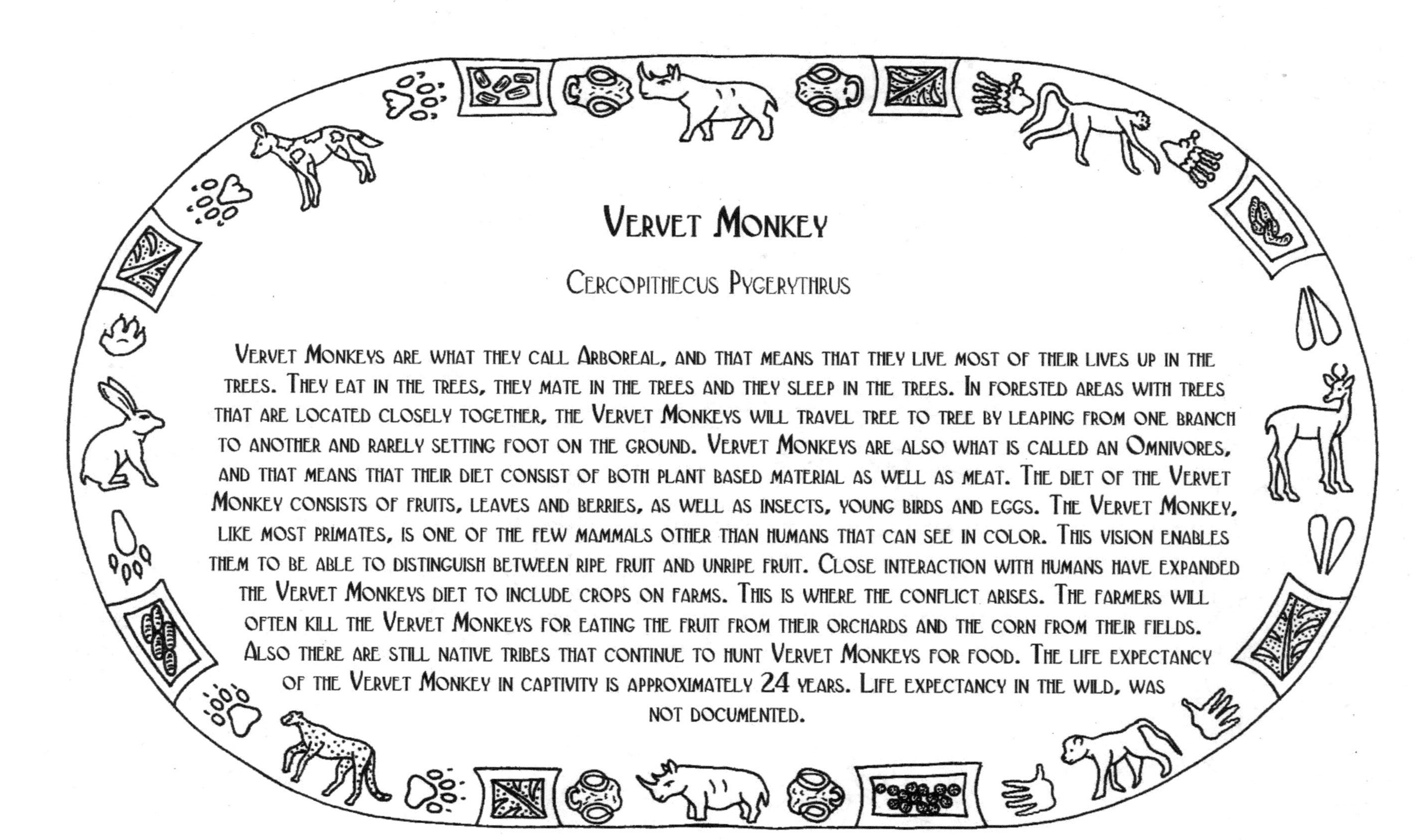

Vervet Monkey

Cercopithecus Pygerythrus

Vervet Monkeys are what they call Arboreal, and that means that they live most of their lives up in the trees. They eat in the trees, they mate in the trees and they sleep in the trees. In forested areas with trees that are located closely together, the Vervet Monkeys will travel tree to tree by leaping from one branch to another and rarely setting foot on the ground. Vervet Monkeys are also what is called an Omnivores, and that means that their diet consist of both plant based material as well as meat. The diet of the Vervet Monkey consists of fruits, leaves and berries, as well as insects, young birds and eggs. The Vervet Monkey, like most primates, is one of the few mammals other than humans that can see in color. This vision enables them to be able to distinguish between ripe fruit and unripe fruit. Close interaction with humans have expanded the Vervet Monkeys diet to include crops on farms. This is where the conflict arises. The farmers will often kill the Vervet Monkeys for eating the fruit from their orchards and the corn from their fields. Also there are still native tribes that continue to hunt Vervet Monkeys for food. The life expectancy of the Vervet Monkey in captivity is approximately 24 years. Life expectancy in the wild, was not documented.

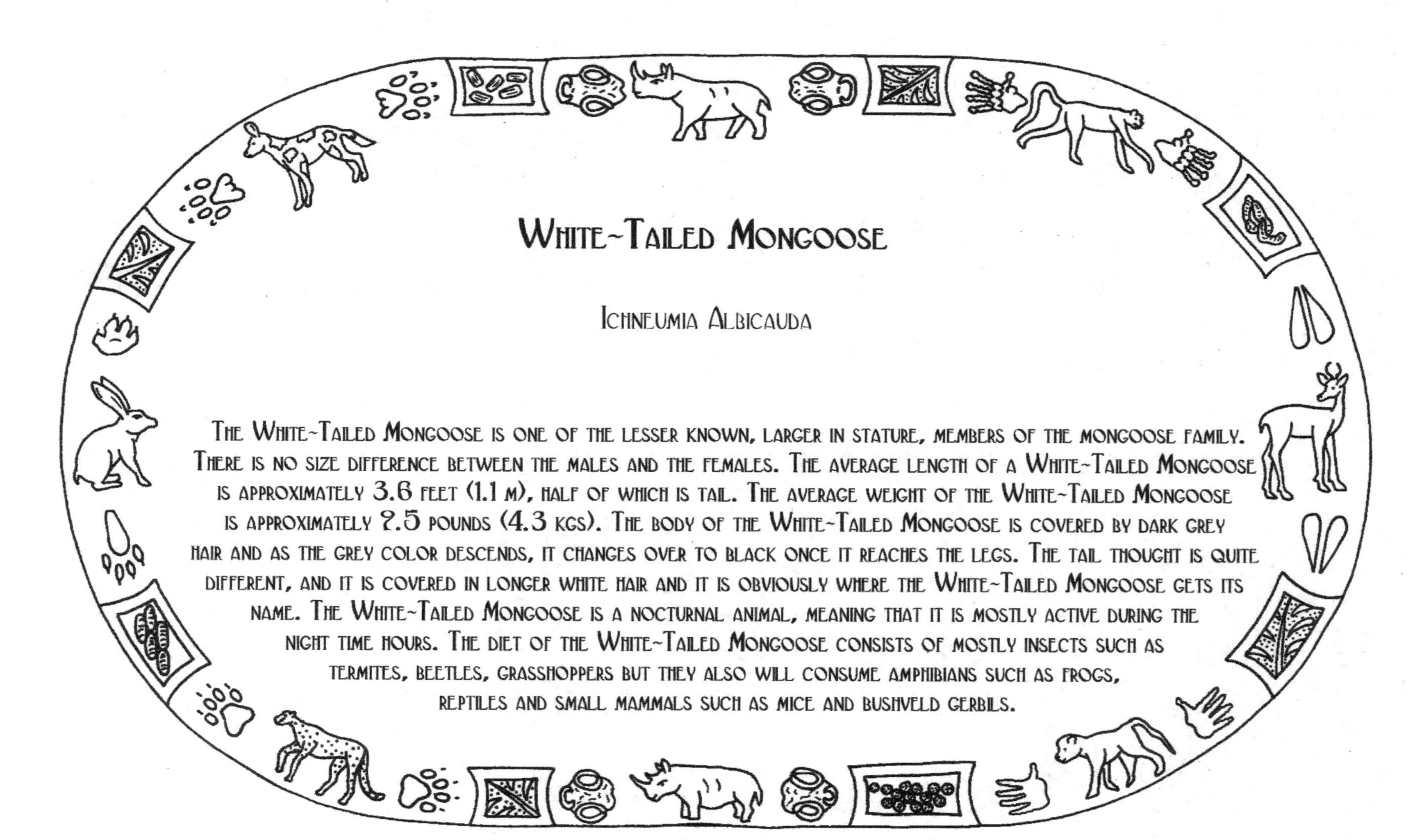

White~Tailed Mongoose

Ichneumia Albicauda

The White~Tailed Mongoose is one of the lesser known, larger in stature, members of the mongoose family. There is no size difference between the males and the females. The average length of a White~Tailed Mongoose is approximately 3.6 feet (1.1 m), half of which is tail. The average weight of the White~Tailed Mongoose is approximately 2.5 pounds (4.3 kgs). The body of the White~Tailed Mongoose is covered by dark grey hair and as the grey color descends, it changes over to black once it reaches the legs. The tail thought is quite different, and it is covered in longer white hair and it is obviously where the White~Tailed Mongoose gets its name. The White~Tailed Mongoose is a nocturnal animal, meaning that it is mostly active during the night time hours. The diet of the White~Tailed Mongoose consists of mostly insects such as termites, beetles, grasshoppers but they also will consume amphibians such as frogs, reptiles and small mammals such as mice and bushveld gerbils.

White-Tailed Mongoose

Ichneumia Albicauda

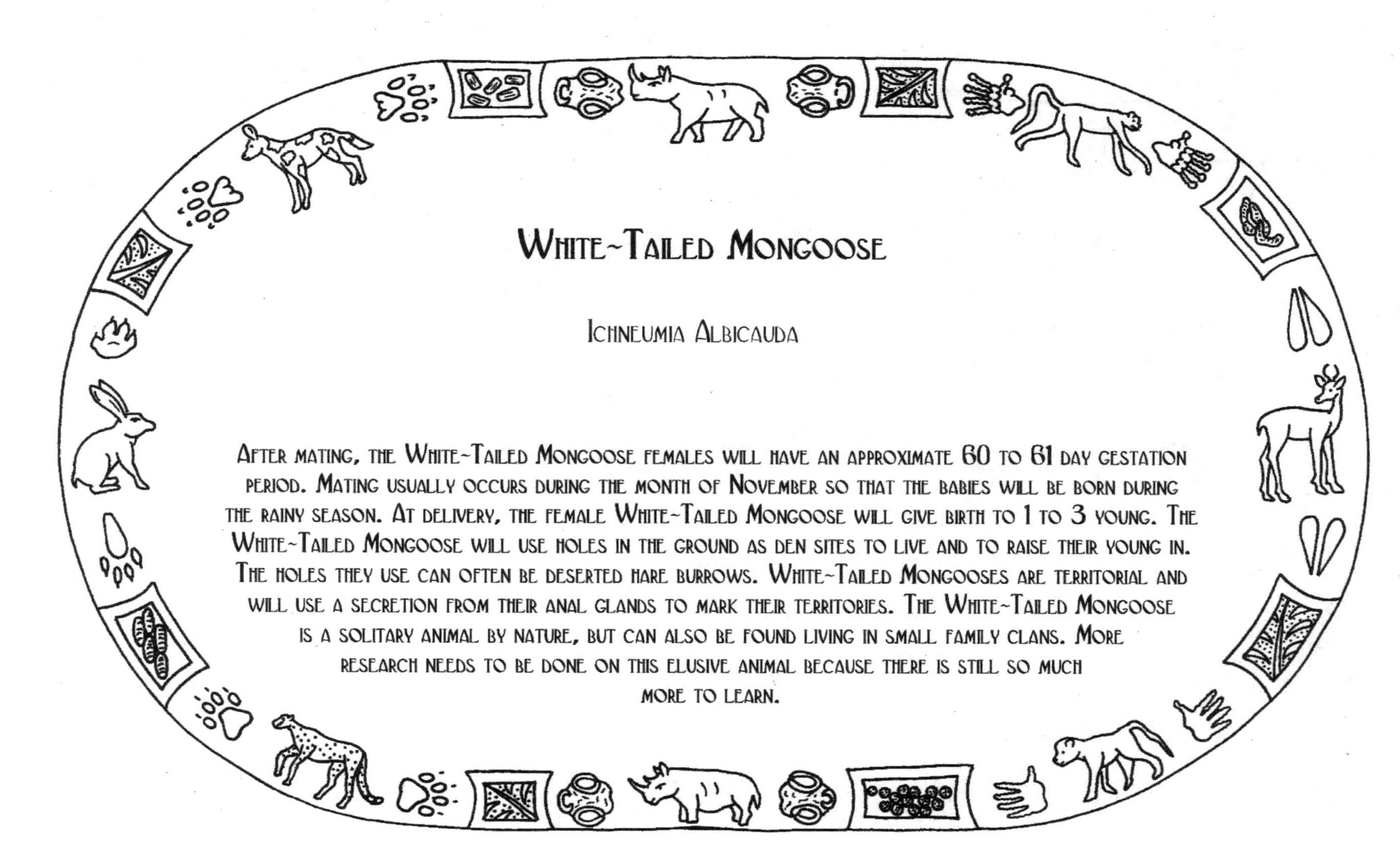

After mating, the White-Tailed Mongoose females will have an approximate 60 to 61 day gestation period. Mating usually occurs during the month of November so that the babies will be born during the rainy season. At delivery, the female White-Tailed Mongoose will give birth to 1 to 3 young. The White-Tailed Mongoose will use holes in the ground as den sites to live and to raise their young in. The holes they use can often be deserted hare burrows. White-Tailed Mongooses are territorial and will use a secretion from their anal glands to mark their territories. The White-Tailed Mongoose is a solitary animal by nature, but can also be found living in small family clans. More research needs to be done on this elusive animal because there is still so much more to learn.

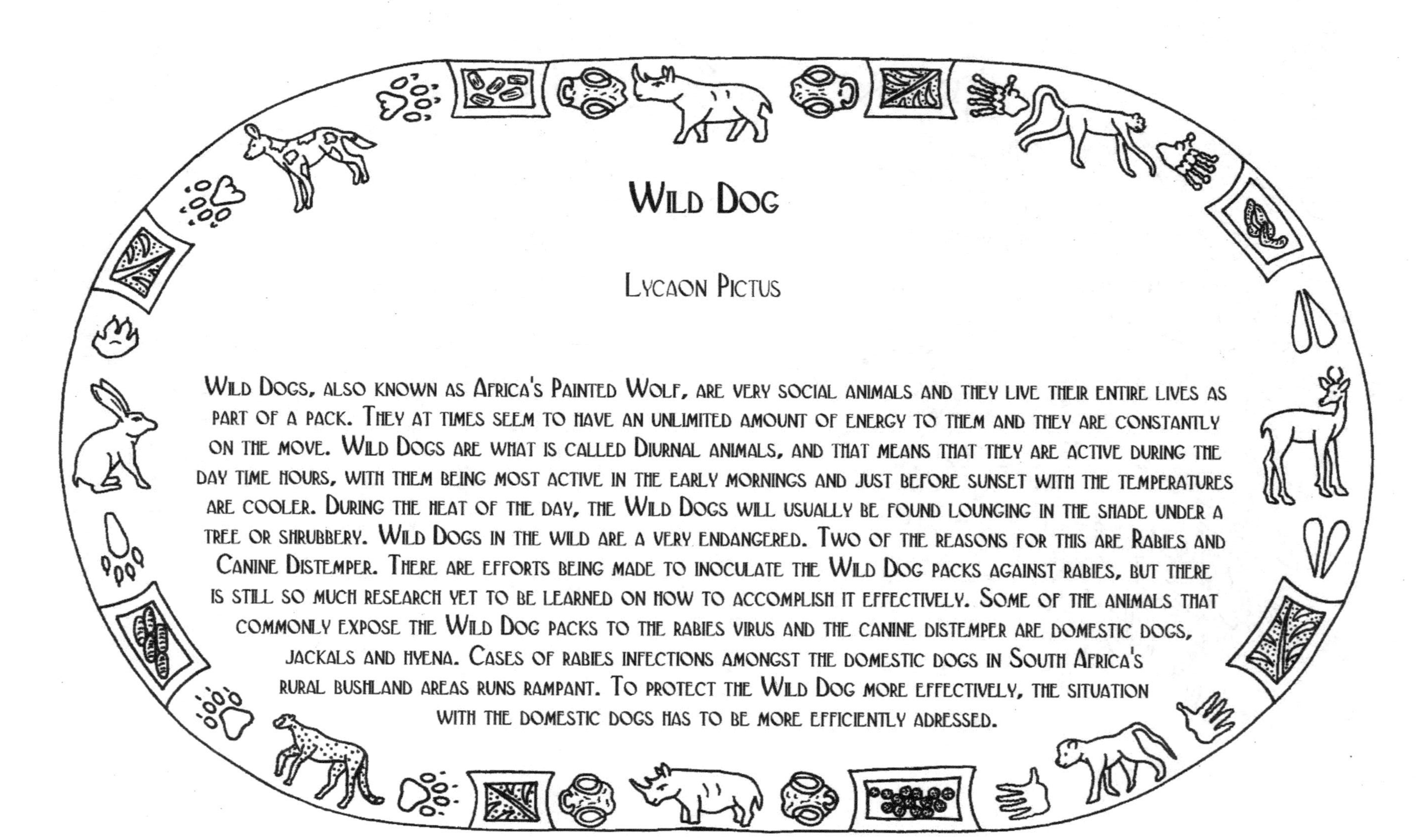

Wild Dog

Lycaon Pictus

Wild Dogs, also known as Africa's Painted Wolf, are very social animals and they live their entire lives as part of a pack. They at times seem to have an unlimited amount of energy to them and they are constantly on the move. Wild Dogs are what is called Diurnal animals, and that means that they are active during the day time hours, with them being most active in the early mornings and just before sunset with the temperatures are cooler. During the heat of the day, the Wild Dogs will usually be found lounging in the shade under a tree or shrubbery. Wild Dogs in the wild are a very endangered. Two of the reasons for this are Rabies and Canine Distemper. There are efforts being made to inoculate the Wild Dog packs against rabies, but there is still so much research yet to be learned on how to accomplish it effectively. Some of the animals that commonly expose the Wild Dog packs to the rabies virus and the canine distemper are domestic dogs, jackals and hyena. Cases of rabies infections amongst the domestic dogs in South Africa's rural bushland areas runs rampant. To protect the Wild Dog more effectively, the situation with the domestic dogs has to be more efficiently adressed.

Wild Dog

Lycaon Pictus

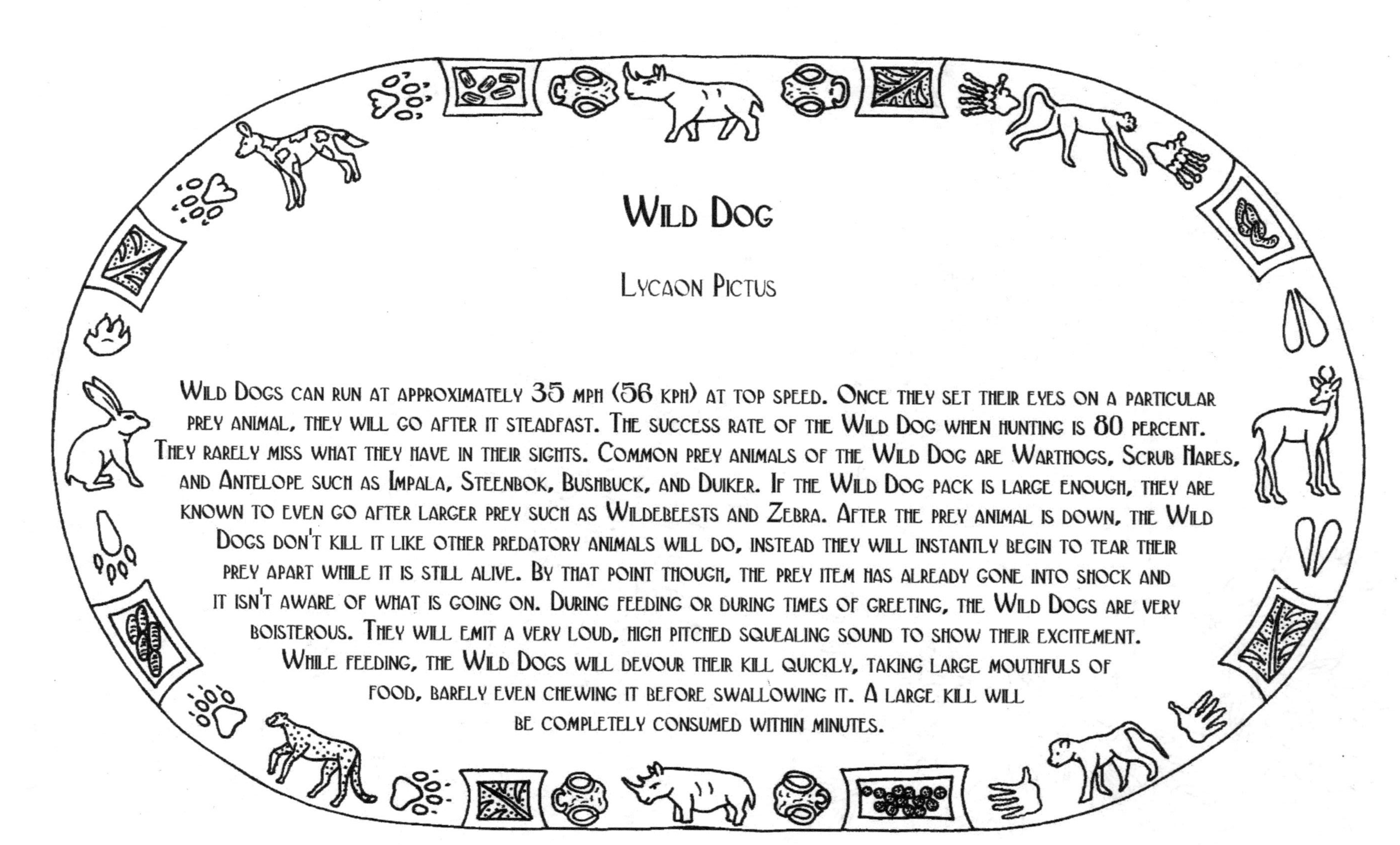

Wild Dogs can run at approximately 35 mph (56 kph) at top speed. Once they set their eyes on a particular prey animal, they will go after it steadfast. The success rate of the Wild Dog when hunting is 80 percent. They rarely miss what they have in their sights. Common prey animals of the Wild Dog are Warthogs, Scrub Hares, and Antelope such as Impala, Steenbok, Bushbuck, and Duiker. If the Wild Dog pack is large enough, they are known to even go after larger prey such as Wildebeests and Zebra. After the prey animal is down, the Wild Dogs don't kill it like other predatory animals will do, instead they will instantly begin to tear their prey apart while it is still alive. By that point though, the prey item has already gone into shock and it isn't aware of what is going on. During feeding or during times of greeting, the Wild Dogs are very boisterous. They will emit a very loud, high pitched squealing sound to show their excitement. While feeding, the Wild Dogs will devour their kill quickly, taking large mouthfuls of food, barely even chewing it before swallowing it. A large kill will be completely consumed within minutes.

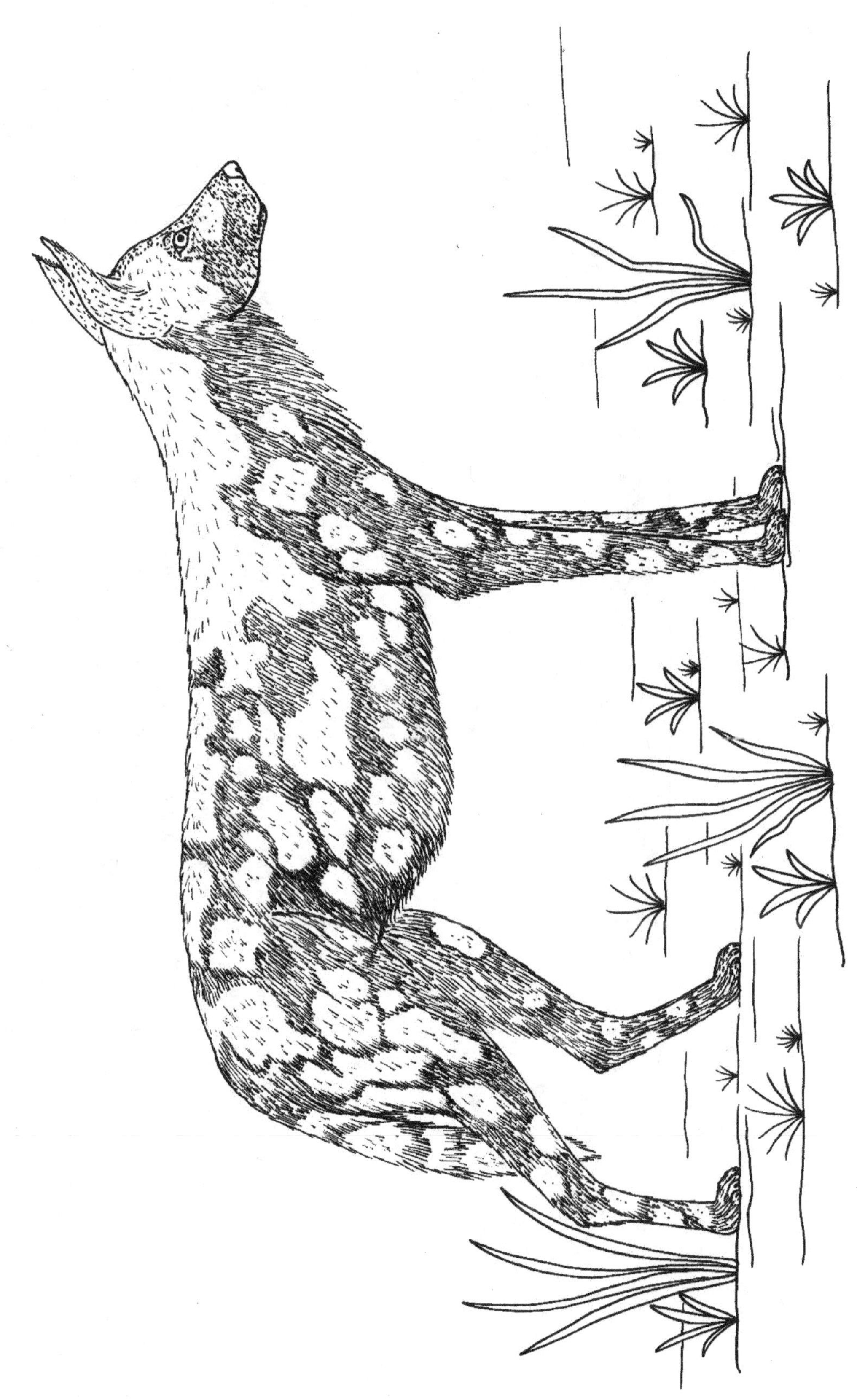

Wild Dog

Lycaon Pictus

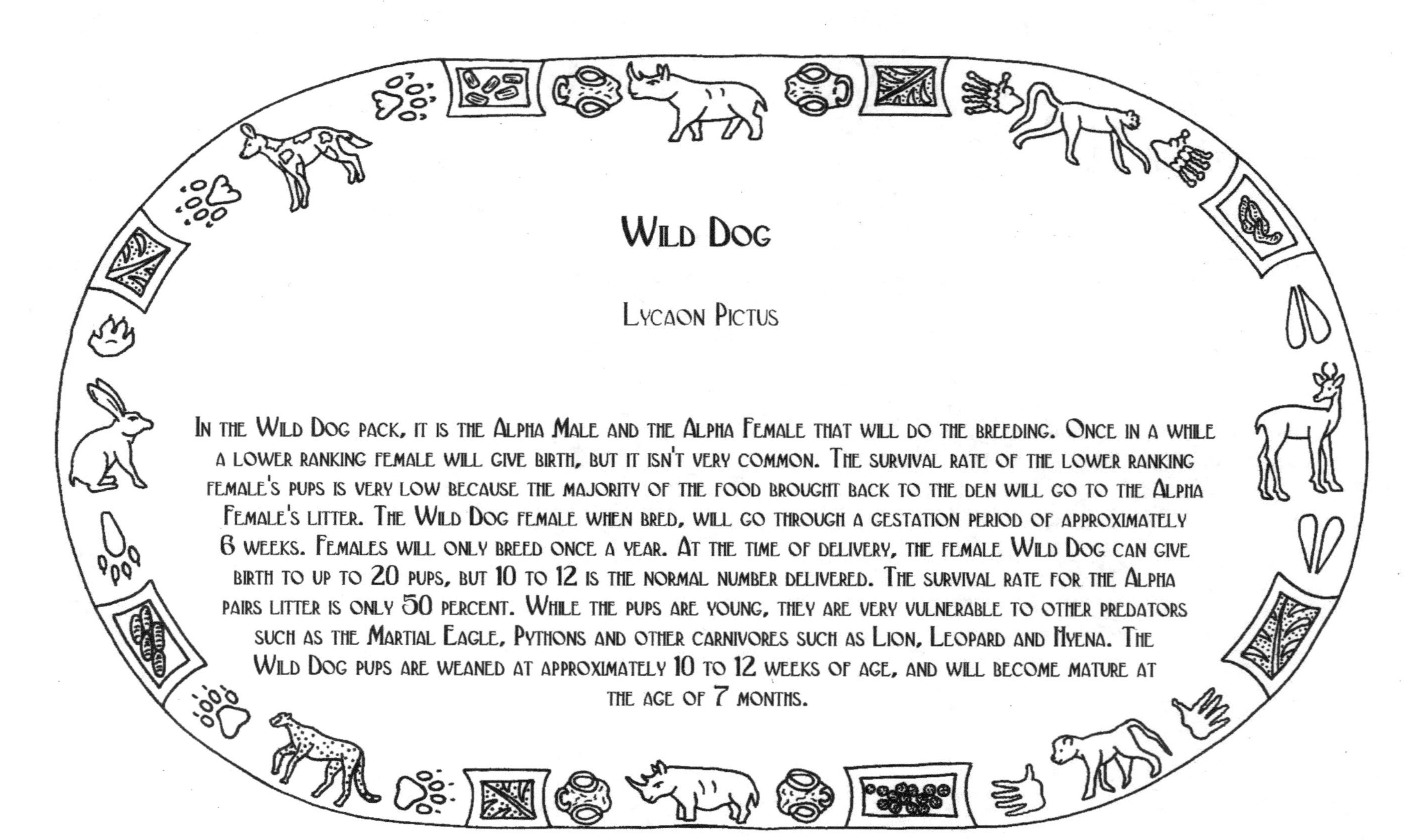

In the Wild Dog pack, it is the Alpha Male and the Alpha Female that will do the breeding. Once in a while a lower ranking female will give birth, but it isn't very common. The survival rate of the lower ranking female's pups is very low because the majority of the food brought back to the den will go to the Alpha Female's litter. The Wild Dog female when bred, will go through a gestation period of approximately 6 weeks. Females will only breed once a year. At the time of delivery, the female Wild Dog can give birth to up to 20 pups, but 10 to 12 is the normal number delivered. The survival rate for the Alpha pairs litter is only 50 percent. While the pups are young, they are very vulnerable to other predators such as the Martial Eagle, Pythons and other carnivores such as Lion, Leopard and Hyena. The Wild Dog pups are weaned at approximately 10 to 12 weeks of age, and will become mature at the age of 7 months.

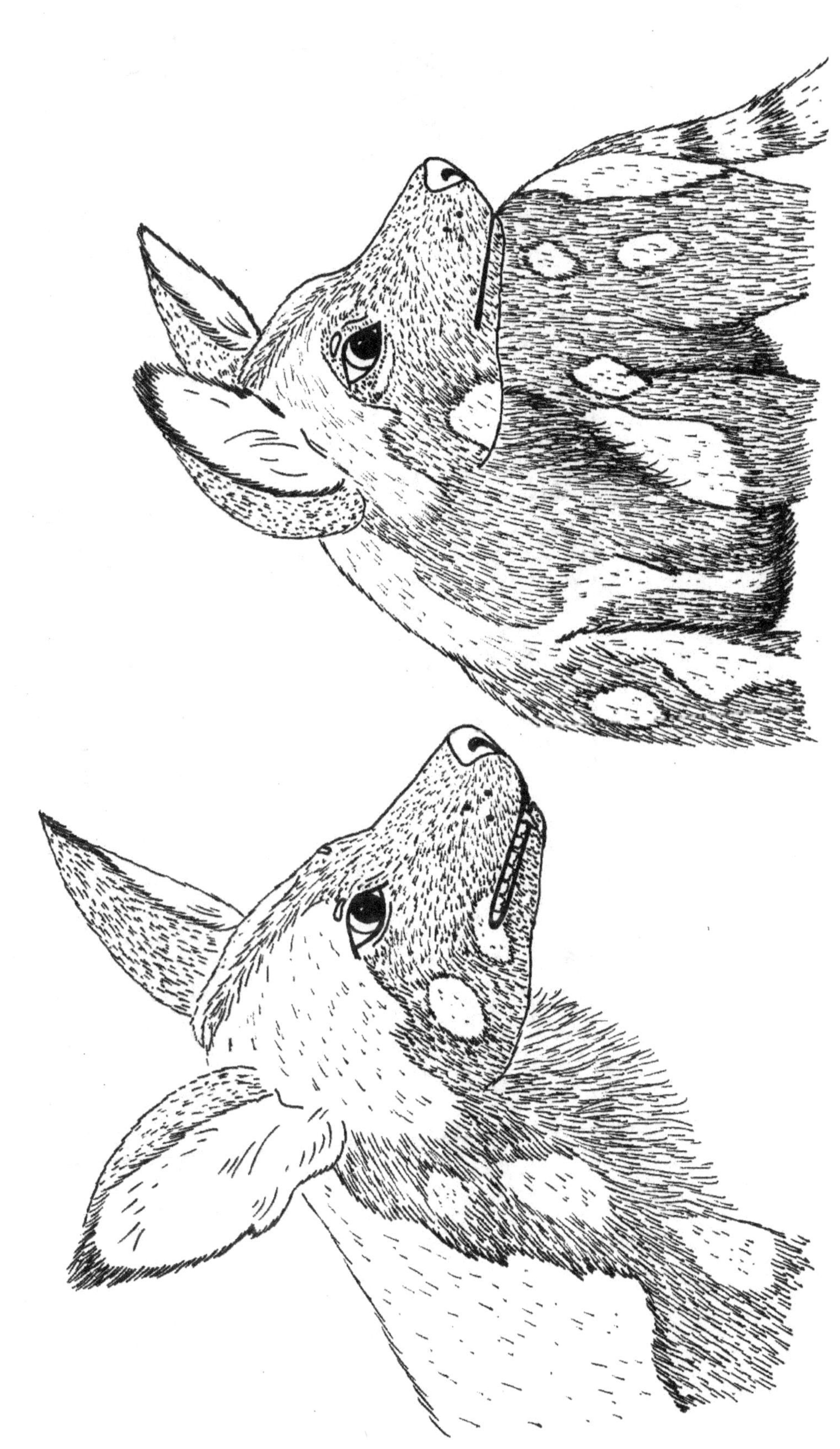

Wild Dog

Lycaon Pictus

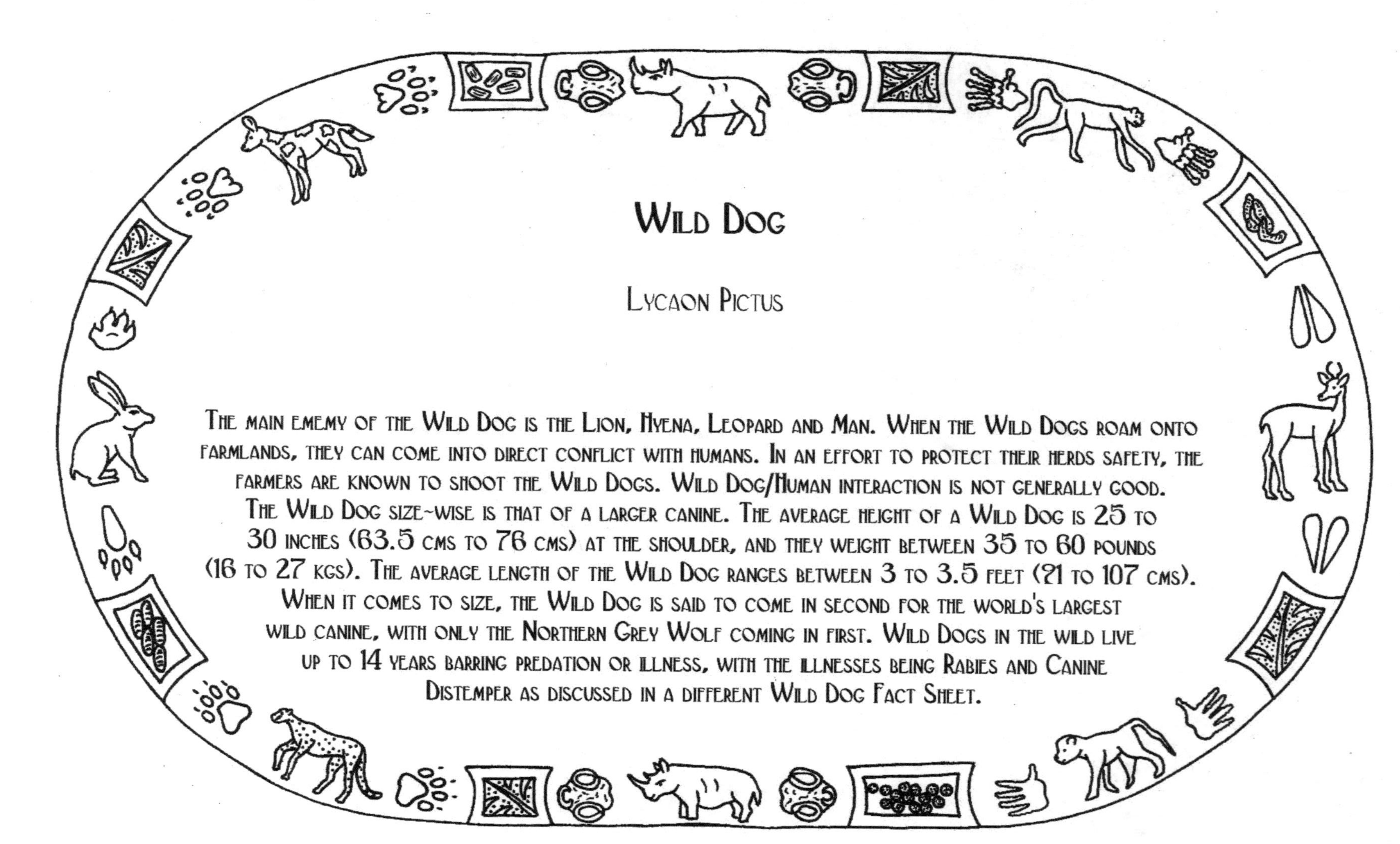

The main ememy of the Wild Dog is the Lion, Hyena, Leopard and Man. When the Wild Dogs roam onto farmlands, they can come into direct conflict with humans. In an effort to protect their herds safety, the farmers are known to shoot the Wild Dogs. Wild Dog/Human interaction is not generally good. The Wild Dog size~wise is that of a larger canine. The average height of a Wild Dog is 25 to 30 inches (63.5 cms to 76 cms) at the shoulder, and they weight between 35 to 60 pounds (16 to 27 kgs). The average length of the Wild Dog ranges between 3 to 3.5 feet (21 to 107 cms). When it comes to size, the Wild Dog is said to come in second for the world's largest wild canine, with only the Northern Grey Wolf coming in first. Wild Dogs in the wild live up to 14 years barring predation or illness, with the illnesses being Rabies and Canine Distemper as discussed in a different Wild Dog Fact Sheet.

9 798686 046955